FRANK MUIR GOES INTO . . . THE ARTS

Based on the popular BBC radio series, this is a
book that will have you laughing out loud. With
the help of Simon Brett, Frank Muir has collected
together jokes, quotes, cartoons and witty press
cuttings on all aspects of the Arts: The visual arts,
books, popular music, serious music, cinema,
television, radio, poetry, conversation and
criticism.

The Third
Frank Muir Goes Into . . .
FRANK MUIR and SIMON BRETT

SPHERE BOOKS LIMITED
30-32 Gray's Inn Road, London WC1X 8JL

First published in Great Britain by Robson Books Ltd 1980
Copyright © 1980 Frank Muir Ltd; and Simon Brett
Published by Sphere Books Ltd 1981

Permissions from hardback edition
Picture sources: Barnaby's Picture Library, The Fotomas Library, Punch,
BBC Photographs, and grateful thanks to the London Library.
Designed by Harold King.
Photographs of Frank Muir by Gemma Levine

TRADE
MARK

Printed and bound in Great Britain by
©ollins, Glasgow

CONTENTS

THE VISUAL ARTS	6
BOOKS	20
POPULAR MUSIC	33
SERIOUS MUSIC	49
CINEMA	62
TELEVISION	78
RADIO	92
POETRY	106
CONVERSATION	119
CRITICISM	133

THE VISUAL ARTS

An artist had just seduced his beautiful young model in his studio. 'Do you know,' he said, 'you're the first model I've ever made love to.'

'I bet,' said the girl. 'Who were your other models?'

'Let me see... A vase of flowers, a melon, a brace of pheasants and a kipper.'

A burglar broke into the house of a modern artist and, while he was stealing all of the valuables, the owner surprised him. Though the burglar got away, the artist had a good look at him and produced a lightning sketch. Police started looking for a man with seven green legs and two poached eggs on his head.

'I'm a Venus de Milo girl,' said the young lady in the back row of the cinema.

'What does that mean?' asked her companion.

'Hands off!'

'Do you know why modern artists sign their paintings at the bottom?'

'No.'

'It's so that you know which way up to hang them.'

My mother-in-law had her photoghraph taken and complained to the photographer that it didn't do her justice.

'You don't need justice,' he said. 'You need mercy.'

A Bohemian artist went to the doctor. After examining him, the doctor said, 'I'll give you a prescription for something to take three times a day with water.'

'What is it?' asked the artist.

'Soap.'

An inexperienced assistant in an art gallery accidentally dropped a priceless painting, tearing the canvas.

'You imbecile!' the Director stormed at him. 'That picture is over four hundred years old.'

'Oh,' said the assistant. 'Lucky it wasn't a new one.'

A beautiful girl went to see an artist. 'Can you paint me in the nude?' she asked.

'Certainly, madam,' he replied. 'But I'll have to keep my socks on – must have somewhere for the brushes.'

A painter's Irish assistant had just finished crating up several valuable pictures for export.

'Now, are you sure you stamped THIS SIDE UP WITH CARE on top of the crate?' asked the painter.

'To be sure I did,' the Irishman replied. 'And, just to be sure, I put it on the bottom as well.'

The World of Art, which this book goes into, is a strange one, because it raises all kinds of problems of definition. Beauty is in the eye of the beholder, and so is art.

The most commonly held view on the subject is, 'I don't know much about Art, but I know what I like' – and it's a view with which one cannot argue. In other words, if you think the plaster ducks on your sitting-room wall are better art than Michelangelo, then that's a perfectly valid artistic judgement. Fortunately, this area of uncertainty about what art is, where it stops and where pretension starts, is fertile ground for humour.

The first art most people think of when the subject's mentioned is painting, but, whatever the art, you're faced with immediate problems of definition. G. K. Chesterton:

> **Art, like morality, consists in drawing the line somewhere.**

More detail on the subject from Dan Rice:

> **There are three forms of visual art: Painting is art to look at, sculpture is art you can walk round, and architecture is art you can walk through.**

Sydney Smith:

> **Painting is an intermediate something between a thought and a thing.**

And how is it done? Here is the opinion of the painter Degas:

> **Painting is easy when you don't know how, but very difficult when you do.**

But none of those definitions help one to spot the genuine from the phoney in the world of art. The person you have condemned as talentless may suddenly be hailed as a genius; there's always an element of uncertainty. James McNeill Whistler:

> **An artist's career always begins tomorrow.**

I suppose ultimately you have to take people at their own valuation. If they say they are artists, they may well be. And if they are, then they have to have all kinds of allowances made for them. Jules Feiffer:

Artists can colour the sky red because they *know* it's blue. Those of us who aren't artists must colour things the way they really are or people might think we're stupid.

And none of us wants to look stupid, particularly in matters of taste. But one must remember to have the confidence that there's no right and wrong in art; just say what you feel; every opinion is equally valid. John White:

There are three kinds of people in the world; those who can't stand Picasso, those who can't stand Raphael, and those who've never heard of either of them.

But, though your personal reaction to art is what matters in the long run, it is possible to be educated in appreciation. Most art teaching begins with the great classical painters, because they seem to strike chords even in the most hardened bosom. Headlines from *The Times Educational Supplement:*

Art for Delinquent Girls. The Taste for Old Masters.

The lives of the great painters of the past are always mistily surrounded in romance. There is a theory that being artistic gives someone the automatic right to be promiscuous – a right claimed by many whose artistic talent is of dubious authenticity. But a certain Bohemianism is expected of painters; sexual misconduct and heavy drinking are *de rigueur*. Here's a clerihew by Allan M. Laing:

**When they found Giotto
blotto,
he said: 'Some twirp's
doped my turps.'**

One from Osbert Mint:

**Toulouse-Lautrec
Was a bit of a wreck,
But his success with women was quite
Exceptional, considering his height.**

" You would like a portrait of your daughter as Ceres, would you not, ma'am ? "

And another from Tom St. Brien:

> **Hans Holbein the Elder**
> **Had a model called Grizelda,**
> **Who produced (according to a scandal-monger)**
> **Hans Holbein the Younger.**

Nowadays we're much less likely to pass judgement on artists' private lives; we're more concerned with their works. But standards vary; there are differences of opinion about the quality of even accepted masterpieces. And often judgement is not helped by the information given in catalogues:

> **On the North Wall there is a large painting of the Trinity**
> **in which the figure of the Almighty is about life-size.**

Just because a painting's famous and acknowledged as a great work of art, you're not bound to like it. Here's Mark Twain on the Mona Lisa:

> **The complexion was bad; in fact it was not even human;**
> **there are no people of that colour.**

But then everyone has the right to say what he likes in an art gallery. Edmond de Goncourt:

> **A painting in a museum hears more ridiculous opinions**
> **than anything else in the world.**

As well as bestowing cultural benefits, art is also a matter of fashion and status. It is chic and financially shrewd to invest in pictures. As a result, not only wealthy individuals, but also wealthy businesses often put their money into art, combining the advantages of respectability and tax concessions. Sometimes the aim is to buy something apposite to the business in question, which leads to advertisements like this one from the *Financial Times:*

> **For sale: 'Beggar Boy' by Murillo. Subject symbolic**
> **investing public, thus suitable boardroom.**

Businesses that don't fancy Old Masters can invest their money in commissioning new works of art to fit their image. Here's a description of a bas-relief, taken from *The Times:*

The design consists of a male and female nude, recumbent but with a suggestion that they are floating in water; thus the main rhythms are not static, but suggest a movement of circulation, appropriate to the transactions of a post office.

'What do they mean PRIVATE view?'

Mind you, if you're going to put public money into art, it's as well to have someone around who understands it. Here's a report from the *Sun* in the late 'sixties:

> **The Prince also commented on three towering sculptures outside the main entrance. Pointing at one which featured a mosaic eye, he asked: 'What the hell's that?'**
> **Salford's mayor, Alderman Edwin Clark, replied: 'It is a remarkable piece of modern sculpture.'**

Sculpture is possibly even more confusing for the uninformed layman than painting. Picking what is good from what is rubbish is extremely difficult and, as increasingly unlikely materials are pressed into the service of art, it doesn't get any easier. The dilemma is illustrated by this report from the *Guardian:*

> **An Argentinian sculptor called Guyla Kosice has just been charged £75 duty by the Customs at London Airport on his 'hydraulic sculptures', because the Customs held that the sculptures – water-filled constructions of plastic which were on their way to be exhibited in London – were not works of art but bits of plumbing.**

The artist in society is doomed to be eternally misunderstood. And, even when he is working in a conventional medium, he is in danger of ridicule. Here's an extract from a letter written to the post-war *Daily Graphic:*

> **My father, Charles Abbey, worked on the Albert Memorial as a sculptor, and said he carved my face among the angels on it. I was a baby at the time. I have often wondered why people run down the beautiful Albert Memorial.**

That's another traditional feature of art – the dedication of the finished creation to a loved one. This can get out of hand, if the loved one is also the medium for the art. A report from the *Daily Mirror:*

> **Over the years I tattooed my wife elaborately. I think some of my finest efforts were dedicated to my wife. I have covered nearly every inch of her body ... Our children ... used to look upon their mother as a fascinating and colourful picture-book and always begged her to show them yet another 'lovely picture' and explain its meaning.**

But nowadays the human body is often an element in works of art. There was an exhibition in London a few years ago in which one work featured a live human breast. The poor girl involved had to lie for hours with her breast protruding through a hole in the structure, while the art-loving public passed by and tittered.

And in Germany a man actually patented himself as a work of art, sat in a cage and charged the public to come and look at him.

In these days, when art can consist of an Andy Warhol soup can or covering two miles of the Australian coastline with sheeting, the horizons for the artist seem to be unlimited. For the amateur art-lover, it is sometimes hard to know who's fooling whom. A report from the old *News Chronicle:*

> **Mr. Green paints in black.**
> **'He has a "thing" about black,' explained Mr. Smith.**
> **Mr. Green calls it an "attachment". His three pictures –**
> **Asphyxiation 1, Asphyxiation 2, and Asphyxiation 3 –**
> **were done on hardboard laid flat on the floor.**
> **'I throw on stove enamel, sand and rubble, put on a pair**
> **of shoes and skid about on it. The marks are funda-**
> **mentally accidental – but interesting.'**

(That, like everything else in art, is no doubt a matter of opinion.)
Coming further up to date, here's a report from the *Guardian* of another artist extending the accepted definition of art:

> **Marioni's own earliest 'sound piece' (which,**
> **incidentally, held an unseen time-element, since it**

Art-Master (who has sent for a cab, pointing to horse). "What do you call that?"
Cabby. "An 'orse, sir." *Art-Master.* "A horse! Rub it out, and do it again!"

involved drinking beer all afternoon beforehand) was the act of urinating into a galvanized bucket from the top of a ten-foot ladder.

The scope for the visual artist was extended by the invention of photography. Not only did it mean that there was no longer such a need for representational painting and open up the possibilities for abstract art, the new invention was also an artistic medium in its own right.

In its early years it was regarded with some suspicion. Here's Ambrose Bierce's definition:

PHOTOGRAPH, n. A picture painted by the sun without instruction in art. It is little better than the work of an Apache, but not quite so good as that of a Cheyenne.

Mark Twain was also a bit wary:

I think a photograph is a most important document, and there is nothing more damning to go down to posterity than a silly, foolish smile caught and fixed forever.

Yes, I think most of us have got a few regrettable snaps around that grin at us idiotically from their albums.

Photography intensified the clash of art against reality, as can be demonstrated by the following famous exchange. An admiring friend looks at a young mother's baby and says:

'My, that's a beautiful baby you have there!'

And the mother replies:

'Oh, that's nothing – you should see his photograph.'

Sometimes photography can improve on reality. It certainly does in the world of fashion. Peter Ustinov:

If Botticelli were alive today, he'd be working for *Vogue*.

Photographers very soon took on the slightly Bohemian, amoral image of other artists. The man in the street remains very wary of anyone who has any connection with the arts. Artists are set apart from the rest of humanity and are not wholly reliable. Here's a poem called 'The Artist' by Sir Walter Raleigh (not, incidentally, the Elizabethan one who prevented royal rising damp, but the scholar and critic who died in 1922):

The Artist and his Luckless Wife
They lead a horrid haunted life,
Surrounded by the things he's made
That are not wanted by the trade.

The world is very fair to see;
The artist will not let it be;
He fiddles with the works of God,
And makes them look uncommon odd.

The Artist is an awful man,
He does not do the things he can;
He does the things he cannot do,
And we attend the private view.

The Artist uses honest paint
To represent things as they ain't,
He then asks money for the time
It took to perpetrate the crime.

And that cynical view of the poor Artist nearly concludes our look at the Visual Arts. But, just to round it off, let's have one more definition from Ambrose Bierce:

PICTURE, n. A representation in two dimensions of something wearisome in three.
Behold great Daubert's picture here on view –
Taken from Life. 'If that description's true,
Grant, heavenly powers, that I be taken too.'

AS USED
BY
H.R.H.
THE
PRINCESS
OF
WALES

HOW TO PROCURE A PHOTOGRAPHIC NEGATIVE

TAKE ANY VILLAGE, AND, IN ITS VICINITY, SELECT A FIELD THROUGH WHICH THERE IS A PUBLIC WAY. FOCUS YOUR VIEW, AND MAKE ALL READY FOR THE NEGATIVE. WHILE THE PROCESS IS GOING ON, TAKE YOUR SEAT UPON THE NEXT STILE [THE MORE DISTANT THE BETTER,] AND LOSE YOUR- SELF IN THE LEADERS OF "THE TIMES". YOU WILL THUS BE GIVING AN OPPORTU- NITY TO CHILDREN OF A SPECULATIVE TURN OF MIND, TO SOLVE THEIR DOUBTS AS TO WHAT YOUR CAMERA REALLY CONTAINS. AT THE EXPIRATION OF 20 MINUTES SHUT UP YOUR TIMES, AND RETURN TO YOUR CAMERA. WHEN YOU TAKE OUT YOUR SLIDE, YOU WILL FIND THAT YOU HAVE SECURED A MOST EXCELLENT NEGATIVE.

BOOKS

'Do you like Kipling?'
    'I don't know. I've never kippled.'

A young man was madly in love with a chorus girl and, as her birthday drew near, he asked her what she'd like as a present. She didn't know. 'How about a book?' he suggested.
    'No, thanks, no. I've got one.'

'Tell me, why did you become a printer?'
    'I just seemed the right type.'

'How is the patient getting on?' the doctor asked the new nurse. 'Have you kept a chart of his progress?'
    'Not exactly, doctor.' she replied, blushing, 'but I can show you my diary.'

Thieves broke into the library of an Irish university professor and stole all his books – including the one he was colouring at the time.

'Morning, Arthur. How are the kids?'
    'Oh, fine, Fred.'
    'How many is it now?'
    'Four.'
    'Going to have any more?'
    'Oh no, the wife says no more.'
    'Why?'
    'Well, she's read this book – says every fifth child born in the world is Chinese.'

A father was telling his son it was about time he got married.
    'But why?' came the reply. 'Why should I buy a book when there's such a good lending library in the town?'

'Are you familiar with Dickens?'
    'Yes, I had tea with him yesterday.'
    'That's ridiculous. Dickens has been dead for over a hundred years.'
    'I thought he was quiet.'

An Irishman saw an advertisement in a newspaper for a book on body-building and sent off for it. Three months later he wrote back to the publishers. 'Dear Sir, I have now read your book. Please send on the muscles by return.'

The M.O. was inspecting a barrack-room and found that one private had a locker full of dirty books. 'Tell me,' he asked, 'are you troubled by sexual fantasies?'
    'Oh no,' said the soldier. 'I quite enjoy them.'

Much-married film star (at her twelfth wedding) to short-sighted old Minister trying to find the marriage ceremony in the prayer book: 'Page 37, darling – take it from the top.'

Most people have come up against books at some time in their lives; compulsory education has made them almost unavoidable. Some people worship them, some hate them.

Here are two who liked to be surrounded by them. First, the Rev. Sydney Smith:

> **No furniture is so charming as books, even if you never open them or read a single word.**

Second, Augustine Birrell:

> **An ordinary man can . . . surround himself with two thousand books . . . and thenceforth have at least one place in the world in which it is possible to be happy.**

Desiderius Erasmus also put them very high on his list of priorities:

> **When I get a little money, I buy books; and if any is left, I buy food and clothes.**

Others prefer to limit their reading. Here's a line from a wonderful elderly character created by Nancy Mitford:

> **I have only read one book in my life and that is 'White Fang'. It's so frightfully good I've never bothered to read another.**

And there are extremists who would burn all books on the grounds that no possible good can come from them. Ambrose Bierce was distrustful of the whole business of writing:

> **INK, n. A villainous compound of taumogallate of iron, gum-arabic and water, chiefly used to facilitate the infection of idiocy and promote intellectual crime.**

But books are also held to be the key to education and, since education is the key to civilisation, they must be available all over the world. Here's a report from *The Times Educational Supplement:*

> **Obsolete text-books are being collected by the education committee from the authority's schools and sent to the English-Speaking Union for distribution to Commonwealth countries where they are urgently needed.**

Unfortunately, it's not only in the Commonwealth that books are scarce. There are so many other distractions nowadays. Leonard Louis Levinson:

> **BOOK – What they make a movie out of for television.**

But, in spite of competition from the more immediate media people do still buy books. There's nothing quite like a good read, and publishers spend a great deal on advertising their wares. Some of their recommendations are a bit bizarre. Here's an advertisement taken from the *Medical Press:*

> **'Failure of the Heart and Circulation' by Terence East, M.A., D.M., F.R.C.P. – This delightful little volume is devoted to problems of central and peripheral circulatory failure . . . It is far too good to miss!**

(Just the thing for a train journey.)

Here's a famous item from a bookseller's list:

> **Shelley – Prometheus Unbound 4/9d. Bound 7/6d.**

And this notice was seen in the window of an enterprising London bookshop:

> **Holy Scripture, Writ Divine,**
> **Leather bound, at one and nine,**
> **Satan trembles when he sees**
> **Bibles sold as cheap as these.**

The trouble with books is that every one of them has an author, and, though some of these are perfectly delightful, others are extremely boring. On the whole, the nastiest things about writers have been said by other writers. Here's a typical generalisation from Oscar Wilde:

In old days books were written by men of letters and read by the public. Nowadays books are written by the public and read by nobody.

A gibe from Austin O'Malley:

It is a mean thief, or a successful author, who plunders the dead.

The charge of plagiarism is one that is always being levelled at writers. Nicholas Chamfort:

Most contemporary books give the impression of having been manufactured in a day, out of books read the day before.

An old anonymous epigram on the same theme:

**Your comedy I've read, my friend,
And like the half you pilfered best.
Be sure the piece you may yet mend,
Take courage, man, and steal the rest.**

And here's a summing-up of the writer's motivation by Montesquieu:

An author is a fool who, not content with having bored those who have lived with him, insists on boring future generations.

The trouble is that most writers put the most interesting parts of themselves into their writing; what's left is what you meet and it's not always as interesting as it thinks it is. Also, writers have a fatal tendency to talk about their work. Benjamin Disraeli:

The author who speaks about his own books is almost as bad as the mother who talks about her own children.

The parallel is quite a common one. I think it was Lord Mancroft who said that publication is for a man what childbirth is for a woman. Authors do tend to have an obsessive interest in their work which is rarely shared by their listeners. The charge of being boring is very often made against writers. Here are a couple more definitions by Ambrose Bierce:

CIRCUMLOCUTION, n. A literary trick whereby the writer who has nothing to say breaks it gently to the reader.

TSETSE FLY, n. An African insect (*Glossina morsitans*) whose bite is commonly regarded as nature's most efficacious remedy for insomnia, though some patients prefer that of the American novelist (*Mendax interminabilis*).

"Unfortunately, I can't remember whether he's a master of the written, spoken, or processed word."

Nowadays a lot of doctors prescribe Sir Walter Scott for insomnia. But that sort of thing is not always an infallible cure, as Heinrich Heine observed:

I fell asleep reading a dull book, and I dreamt that I was reading on, so I awoke from sheer boredom.

It's difficult to know the best approach to reading a really dull book, but here's an idea from a wartime *Evening Standard* that might come in useful:

> **Major Smalley will begin a book at the last line of the last page, reading through to the front, holding the book upside down. It takes him no longer than the normal way of reading, and he claims it gives printed matter freshness.**

Authors rarely get to know what the reading public think of their books – or indeed which way up they are read – but they are left in no doubt of the opinions of critics. Some criticisms can be very wounding. Here's a good general attack from Charles Dickens:

> **There are books of which the backs and covers are by far the best parts.**

A bit more demolition work from Rose Macaulay:

> **It was a book to kill time for those who liked it better dead.**

Will Cuppy:

> ***Sartor Resartus* is simply unreadable, and for me that always sort of spoils a book.**

Mark Twain:

> **[The Mormon Bible] is chloroform in print. If Joseph Smith composed this book, the act was a miracle – keeping awake while he did it was, at any rate.**

And George De Witt:

> **His books are selling like wildfire. Everybody's burning them.**

Another way of diminishing a writer is by drawing attention to his lack of success. It may be true, as it has been said, that everybody has a novel in them, but would all those novels have readers? Readers are absolutely vital to a writer. A comment on an author by Stanley Walker:

He was an author whose works were so little known as to be almost confidential.

And another from Franklin Pierce Adams:

A first edition of his work is a rarity, but a second is rarer still.

In some literary circles those remarks would be taken as compliments. There is a feeling that a novelist should be a misunderstood martyr to his art, and that popularity breeds contempt. A true novel, some say, is above such minor considerations as readers. After all, think of Mark Twain's definition of a Classic:

A book which people praise but don't read.

There is a great cultural divide between art and rubbish in books, but a simple rule of thumb to distinguish them is that rubbish is what people read. H. L. Mencken:

In the main, there are two sorts of books: those that no one reads and those that no one ought to read.

DOCTOR SYNTAX READING HIS TOUR

But there's nothing wrong with reading rubbish, if that's what you enjoy. And at times we all need a good rubbishy book to settle down with. A shrewd observation from G. K. Chesterton:

> **There is a great deal of difference between the eager man who wants to read a book and the tired man who wants a book to read.**

There are plenty available in the second category, as Charles Colton observed:

> **Many books require no thought from those who read them, and for a very simple reason – they made no such demand upon those who wrote them.**

And often those are the books that sell. Many highly intelligent authors have realised this and adjusted their style accordingly. It makes good economic sense. Mark Twain:

> **My books are water: those of great geniuses are wine. Everybody drinks water.**

The author who can mix water to the public taste does very well. There are all those possible film rights for the best-seller, all those translation rights and serial rights. But some people don't like serials. Among them was Ambrose Bierce, who seems to have had a rather cynical attitude to most aspects of literature:

> **SERIAL, n. A literary work, usually a story that is not true, creeping through several issues of a newspaper or magazine. Frequently appended to each instalment is a 'synopsis of preceding chapters' for those who have not read them, but direr need is a synopsis of succeeding chapters for people who do not intend to read them. A synopsis of the entire work would be still better.**
>
> **(The late James F. Bowman was writing a serial tale for a weekly paper in collaboration with a genius whose name has not come down to us. They wrote, not jointly, but alternately, Bowman supplying the instalment for one week, his friend for the next, and so on, world without end, they hoped.**
> **Unfortunately they quarrelled, and one Monday morning when Bowman read the paper to prepare**

himself for the task, he found his work cut out for him in a way to surprise and pain him. His collaborator had embarked every character of the narrative on a ship and sunk them all in the deepest part of the Atlantic!)

Authors often have difficulty in finding out exactly how well their works are selling. But there are other ways of gauging success. Here's a useful guide from Robert Benchley:

I have been told by hospital authorities that more copies of *my* works are left behind by departing patients than those of any other author.

CARTER'S
LITERARY MACHINE
(PATENTED)

For holding a book or writing-desk. lamp, &c., in any position, over an easy chair, bed, or sofa, obviating the fatigue and inconvenience of incessant stooping while reading or writing. Invaluable to invalids and students. Admirably adapted for India. A most useful gift. PRICES From £1 1s. Illustrated Price List Post Free.

One perennially popular form of fiction is the detective story or 'whodunnit', now often graced with the more elegant title of crime novel. In the old days these stories had fixed rules and plots you could set your watch by. They existed in a world which enabled J. B. Morton to come up with this definition:

LIBRARY: The room where the murders take place.

Now the old order is changing and not, I fear, for the better. From a book review in the *Church Times:*

Turning to crime stories proper, we regret to note that murder seems to be losing all association with refinement.

... " *This looks to me like ' Dead-Face ' Anderson's work,*" *gasped Derective- Inspector Watkins, eyeing the corpse in the bath. . . .*"

Yes, there has been a definite literary shift amongst murderers from the aristocratic to the criminal classes. Not that it probably makes much difference to the average detective story addict – or to those who can't stand the genre. Here's part of a letter sent to the *Daily Mirror:*

> **I spend hours at the local library reading detective stories. But I read only the first and last chapters of each. The only time I read one right through I got so bored that I didn't care who had committed the murder.**

And before the readers of this chapter get too bored to care, I'll finish our investigation into books with an anonymous epitaph on an author:

> **I suffered so much from printer's errors**
> **That death for me can hold no terrors;**
> **I'll bet this stone has been misdated,**
> **I wish to God I'd been cremated.**

POPULAR MUSIC

The bass-player turned to the drummer during a concert. 'Keep on playing,' he said. 'I'm just going out to see what the band sounds like.'

A long-haired pop star was having his hair cut. After about half an hour the barber said, 'Good Lord, I didn't know you went to Winchester.'
   'How do you know?' asked the pop star.
   'I've just got to your cap.'

'And now, ladies and gentlemen,I would like to give you "The Perambulator Song".'
   '"The Perambulator Song"? How does it go?'
   'It doesn't go. You push it! Or perhaps you'd like a different one... How about "The Prune Song"?'
   '"The Prune Song"? How does it go?'
   'Very regularly.'

A band-leader was bawling out a banjo-player. 'That instrument isn't even in tune,' he shouted.
   'That's funny,' said the banjo-player. 'It was when I bought it.'

FAVOURITE SONG TITLES:

She was only a lamplighter's daughter, but she went out every night.

She was only an architect's daughter, but she let the borough surveyor.

A drummer arrived at the dance hall and found that none of the rest of the band had turned up. Being a professional, he played on his own and the people danced away without paying too much attention to him. At last a woman came up to him and said, 'Excuse me, but please could you play "Whispering"?'
   'Oh blimey,' said the drummer. 'That's what I've been playing all evening.'

'What's a sea shanty?'

'It's what you pay £45 a week for when you rent a bungalow at Margate.'

'What's black and bumps into pianos?'

'Ray Charles.'

A busker wandered into a village one Sunday morning while everyone was in church, so he decided to play until they all came out. The noise caused some distraction and eventually the vicar came out of the church shouting, 'Do you know you're interrupting the service?'

'No, I don't,' replied the busker, 'but you sing it, I'll play it.'

An Irishman went into a record shop and asked the girl behind the counter for 'Rhapsody in Blue'. She said they hadn't got it.

'Well, would you mind having another look?' asked the customer. 'Perhaps they do it in some other colour?'

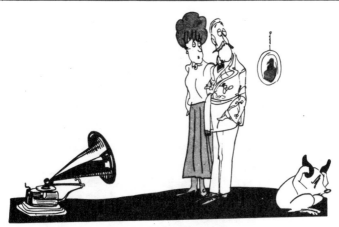

"I think he's gone off John McCormack."

Dividing music into two categories, Popular and Serious, is a false distinction, because the popular music of one period can become the classical music of another, and some musical works defy such glib definition. But it's a convenient device for this book, because the humour of the popular music business is very different from the humour of pretension which surrounds serious music.

Noël Coward commented on the potency of cheap music and few of us can live our lives unaffected by it. Even if we never listen to the current product, we still find our newspapers full of its trivia, the stories of pop stars' romances and so on. Even a staid journal like *The Times* contains pop criticism and includes pop stars in its birthdays column. (They're the depressing ones with ages under thirty.)

Popular music is an inescapable part of life and always has been. It's foolish to despise it just because it's popular. Here's Irving Berlin's advice to Cole Porter:

Listen, kid, take my advice, never hate a song that has sold a half-million copies!

But a lot of people do manage to hate it, nonetheless. Here's James Agee on the subject of Hollywood musicals:

If music be the breakfast food of love, kindly do not disturb until lunch-time.

And another reworking of the same quote by D. J. Hurst:

If music be the food of love, why don't rabbits sing?

Whatever popular music's like, it is always accused of triviality. In the same way that the highbrow is suspicious of a best-selling book, he is wary of a popular tune, however catchy. Often it's the immediacy of a tune's appeal that puts people off; enjoyment, they think, can't be that simple. Here's Mark Twain's view:

I suppose there are two kinds of music – one kind which one feels just as an oyster might, and another sort which requires a higher faculty, a faculty which must be assisted and developed by teaching. Yet if base music gives certain of us wings, why should we want any other?

I suppose it's really a question of how base the music is. The values of the pop world can be dubious. Brad Anderson:

I've never heard such corny lyrics, such simpering sentimentality, such repetitious, uninspired melody. Man, we've got a hit on our hands!

The pop industry does have a slightly seedy image, apparently even for cows, if we are to believe this letter, written to the *Radio Times* in the 'forties:

> **We find that our cows give their highest milk yields to the strains of eighteenth-century chamber music, such as Haydn quartets. Music in the modern idiom often calms them into lying down at the wrong time: 'swing' definitely creates a 'kicking the bucket' tendency.**

This disapproval of the popular is even more evident in church music. Though trendy vicars may hold their teenybopper masses and London theatres be full of God-rock musicals, most church-goers favour the traditional and have strong views on what is proper. Here's a report from the *Scottish Daily Express:*

> **When 'Three Blind Mice' rang out from the belfry of Great Cornard (Suffolk) Parish Church, the bellringer was warned against such levity. Then one Sunday there was a very poor offertory and from the belfry came 'Put Another Nickel In'. The bellringer has been sacked.**

Yes, it's rarely that popular music is treated with respect, though it does happen. The Beatles, of course, were accorded serious critical consideration. Tony Palmer described Lennon and McCartney as the greatest songwriters since Schubert, and one LP received this encomium in the *New Statesman:*

> **The best songs for me are the love songs in which lyrical pentatonic innocence is modified but not destroyed by rhythmic ellipsis or harmonic ambiguity.**

Styles in popular music change faster and faster. Every week the new group is launched that is going to revolutionise the scene, and every week after it's forgotten.

There has always been a lot of change in popular music, but what really speeded the process up was the invention of sound recording. Let's have a definition from someone who was around during its infancy – Ambrose Bierce:

> **PHONOGRAPH, n. An irritating toy that restores life to dead noises.**

I think it's probably as well that he didn't live to see how much the gramophone record was going to take over people's life. I can't imagine Bierce enjoying disc jockeys. But that sort of music programme is now one of the staples of broadcasting and it has introduced a new game of oneupmanship, in which people vie to get their requests played on the radio by their favourite disc jockey. Letters for such requests should be written with care. Here are a few examples of ones that weren't:

> **Please could you play a record of your choice for my Mum and Dad, sister Maureen, brother Lionel, husband Terry and son Paul, all of whom have a birthday this year.**

> **Could you play me 'Stranger on the Shore' before ten o'clock in the morning and could you please play it quietly because my husband works nights.**

> **Could you play Engelbert Humperdinck's 'Please Release Me', because it has sentimental associations for my husband, who hopes to be back with us soon.**

The trouble is that getting your record played may not be the end of your problems. A letter sent to the *Daily Mirror:*

> **I know what a thrill it is to hear one's request record played on the radio. I had my request played after plaguing the BBC for seventeen years. Unfortunately I was so excited that I cried all the time the record was on the air and I didn't hear a note of it!**

Another form in which popular music is presented to the public is as an accompaniment to dancing and new dances are constantly being invented. As soon as they are invented, they are condemned by contemporary opinion. The eighteenth century reeled at the audaciousness of the waltz, and more recent examples have set off similar shock-waves. A report from a wartime *Daily Mirror:*

> **We were shocked and surprised to hear, on Sunday evening, broadcast from Paris what purports to be a new dance called 'Le Chamberlain'.**
> **This dance apparently involves the use of an umbrella, and we think you will agree with us that, in times like these, our beloved Premier should be spared such exhibitions of bad taste.**

MUSIC-HALL INANITIES.—I.

Miss Birdie Vandeleur ("Society's Pet"—vide her advertisements passim) bawls the refrain of her latest song :—

"Ow, I am sow orferly *shy*, boys!
I am, and I kennot tell wy, boys!
Some dy, wen I'm owlder,
Per'aps I'll git bowlder,
But naow I am **orfer**-ly shy!"

'E's not a *tall* man— Nor a *short* man— But he's just the man for me.'

' Not in the army— Nor the nivy— But the royal artill-er-ee !

MUSIC-HALL INANITIES.—II. The Illustrative Method

The great thing about dancing is that it's a participant activity and lots of people want to participate in music, not just to listen to it. The result prompted this remark from George Bernard Shaw:

Hell is full of musical amateurs.

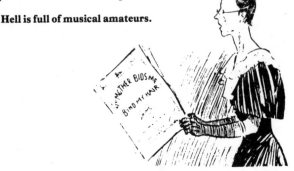

Musical amateurs love to have a go, regardless of talent. Some of them see themselves as vocalists. A famous anonymous limerick:

> **There was an old fellow of Tring**
> **Who, when somebody asked him to sing,**
> > **Replied, 'Ain't it odd?**
> > **I can never tell "God**
> **Save the Weasel" from "Pop Goes the King".'**

No doubt it was of such a performer that Samuel Taylor Coleridge wrote this epigram:

> **Swans sing before they die – 'twere no bad thing**
> **Should certain persons die before they sing.**

Other amateurs fancy themselves as instrumentalists. On the violin, perhaps. Here's an anonymous eighteenth-century verse – 'To a Bad Fiddler':

> **Old Orpheus played so well, he mov'd Old Nick,**
> **While thou mov'st nothing but thy fiddle-stick.**

Or maybe they prefer the piano, defined thus by Ambrose Bierce:

> **PIANO, n. A parlour utensil for subduing the impenitent**
> **visitor. It is operated by depressing the keys of the**
> **machine and the spirits of the audience.**

45

But shortcomings in talent can be balanced by enthusiasm. And the thrill of performing in public. If you're lucky, the local press will be there to review the performance and give you one of those cuttings that all artists treasure. Like this one, from a Sunday paper:

> **Music was provided by the pipe band of Queen Victoria School and the brass band of the first Battalion Gordon Highlanders. There was a complete absence of wind.**

Or this, from South Africa:

> **The concert held in the Good Templars' Hall was a great success ... Special thanks are due to the Vicar's daughter who laboured the whole evening at the piano, which as usual fell upon her.**

And, finally, a report all the way from Massachusetts:

> **Not to be outdone by other artists, John Totten and his banjo, along with several friends and their banjos, will provide an instrumental interlude, which itself should be worth the price of admission (which by the way is free).**

But let us for a moment leave this triviality and concentrate on the real power of music. Have your handkerchiefs ready as you read a moving ballad by Scotland's own Poet and Tragedian, William McGonagall. It's called 'Saved by Music':

> At one time, in America, many years ago,
> Large gray wolves were wont to wander to and fro;
> And from the farm yards they carried pigs and calves
>   away,
> Which they devoured ravenously, without dismay.
>
> But, as the story goes, there was a negro fiddler called
>   old Dick,
> Who was invited by a wedding party to give them music,
> In the winter time, when the snow lay thick upon the
>   ground,
> And the rivers far and near were frozen all around.
>
> And when hurrying onward, not to be late at the
>   festival,
> He heard the howl of a wolf, which did his heart appal,
> And the howl was answered, and as the howl came near,
> Poor old Dick, fiddle in hand, began to shake with fear.
>
> And as the wolves gathered in packs from far and near,
> Old Dick in the crackling bushes did them hear,
> And they ran along to keep pace with him,
> Then poor Dick began to see the danger he was in.
>
> He remembered an old hut stood in the clearing,
> And towards it he was slowly nearing,
> And the hope of reaching it urged him on,
> But he felt a trifle dispirited and woe-begone.
>
> And the poor fellow's heart with fear gave a bound,
> When he saw the wolves' green eyes glaring all around,
> And they rushed at him boldly, one after another,
> Snapping as they passed, which to him was great bother.
>
> For the wolves pursued him without delay,
> But Dick arrived at the hut in great dismay,
> And had just time to get on the roof and play,
> And at the strains of the music the wolves felt gay.

And for several hours he sat there in pain,
Knowing if he stopped playing the wolves would be at
    him again,
But the rage of the wolves abated to the subduing
    strains,
And at last he was rewarded for all his pains:

For the wedding-party began to weary for some music,
And they all came out to look for old Dick,
And on the top of the hut they found him fiddling away,
And they released him from his dangerous position
    without delay.

Popular music has always had that kind of potency, though the victims of its hypnotic powers tend nowadays to be teenage girls rather than wolves. It's for them the pop idols are created. And woe betide the adult who says all pop idols are alike. At least the stars themselves know their own styles. Here's an extract from an interview with erstwhile pop hero, Terry Dene, published in the *Daily Mail:*

> 'Terry, what's the difference between your act and Tommy Steele's?'
> 'Tommy is more of a happy singer, more merry-like. I do more of a jerk. I jerk a lot, whereas Tommy is happy-go-lucky. I prefer a serious face mostly.'

And, so long as such distinctions are maintained, the future of popular music is assured.

SERIOUS MUSIC

'What's on the festival programme for this evening?'
  'It's most unusual – there's the Limerick String Quartet.'
  'What's unusual about that?'
  'There are six members.'

In a packed Albert Hall for the Proms a lot of jostling was inevitable and one promenader, after being thumped in the back, turned and said, 'Here, who do you think you're pushing?'
  'I don't know,' said the man behind. 'What's your name?'

An American conductor was so outraged when a woodwind player ruined a quiet passage that he shot the man, and was sent to the electric chair for his crime. The lever was pulled three times, but the murderer survived, because he was such a bad conductor.

A psychiatrist went to see a man who thought he was Johann Sebastian Bach. 'I hear you're Johann Sebastian Bach,' he said.
  'That's right. Want to hear me play?' The man sat down at the piano and gave a passable rendition of 'Chopsticks'.
  'Very good indeed,' said the psychiatrist. 'Now I'd like to hear your "Toccata in D Minor".'
  'What?' snapped the man. 'Again?'

'Excuse me, record shop assistant, have you got "Greensleeves"?'
  'No, sir, it's the fluorescent lighting that does it.'

I was once lost in London. Just off the Cromwell Road, I saw a chap walking along with a violin case under his arm. I said to him, 'Excuse me, how do I get to the Albert Hall?'
  'Practice, my boy, years of practice.'

'Doctor, doctor, come quickly. My husband's broken a leg.'
  'But I'm a doctor of music.'
  'That's all right. It's the leg of the piano.'

Two girls were talking about their piano playing. 'Oh yes,' says one, 'when I'm asked to play something, I never make excuses or say I can't play. I just sit straight down at the piano.'

'Yes,' says the other, 'much nicer to let people find out for themselves, isn't it?'

Music, they say, hath charms to soothe the savage breast and there are well-authenticated cases of animals being charmed by it. A musician once went out into darkest Africa to test this theory. He set up his music stand in a jungle clearing and started to play the violin.

The effect was amazing. The birds ceased to chirrup, the monkeys stopped chattering, the lions stopped roaring and all the animals in the jungle came slowly into the clearing and sat down to listen. All was peace – nothing could be heard but the violin's beautiful music.

Then an old crocodile came lumbering out of the river, through the trees, went right up to the musician, opened its jaws and ate him. All the animals was furious.

'Hey,' shouted the lion. 'We were enjoying the music. What did you do that for?'

And the crocodile said, 'Eh?'

In most instances Serious Music is easily distinguishable from Popular Music. Often it's the work of composers long dead, which has stood the test of time; that's called Classical Music. A quick definition from Kin Hubbard:

Classical music is the kind we keep hoping will turn into a tune.

Modern Serious Music differs from that only in that it makes no attempt to turn into a tune. Jascha Heifetz:

I occasionally play works by contemporary composers and for two reaons. First to discourage the composer from writing any more and secondly to remind myself how much I appreciate Beethoven.

Music of every sort is a great solace to many people, and categorising it is made difficult by the fact that much Serious Music is very popular, though it still retains a distinct identity from Popular Music. But don't let's get bogged down in definitions; let's consult a music-lover, the Rev. Sydney Smith:

If I were to begin life again, I would devote it to music. It is the only cheap and unpunished rapture upon earth.

Here's more grudging praise from Dr. Johnson:

Of all noises I think music the least disagreeable.

The trouble is that, despite their enthusiasm for music, the British are not held to be a very musical race. This paradox was expressed succintly by Sir Thomas Beecham:

The English may not like music, but they absolutely love the sound it makes.

As well as bringing consolation to the lonely soul, music can have more public overtones. The works of certain composers have been identified with certain political views, and in times of war music may be condemned simply on grounds of nationality. Here are some examples of British hypersensitivity during the last war. First, from the *Daily Herald:*

> **As Burgomaster Oud, of Rotterdam, was escorted to his seat at a Plymouth cinema for a special showing of 'The Way We Live', stage amplifiers blared unfamiliar music.**
>
> **The Lord Mayor, who accompanied the Burgomaster, thought it might be the Dutch National Anthem, and stood to attention. The audience followed suit. So did the Burgomaster. And nobody knew that the music to which they had paid homage was German – a Mozart overture.**

THE BRITISH CHARACTER.
FAILURE TO APPRECIATE GOOD MUSIC.

Another, from the same paper:

> **The BBC has cancelled the performance of Puccini's opera 'Madam Butterfly', which was to have been given next Wednesday. No reason is given officially. But it is the BBC's way of showing disapproval of Japan's aggression.**

And the *Croydon Times:*

> **Strict impartiality is reflected in the choice of works for performance at the London Philharmonic Orchestra's concerts at the Davis. In December the main work on the programme was the Second Symphony of Sibelius, greatest Finnish composer. Last Sunday the principal work was the Fifth Symphony of Tschaikowsky, greatest Russian composer. In fairness to the memory of Tschaikowsky, it should be emphasised that his music was the product of Tsarist and not Bolshevist Russia.**

Even without making political *faux pas* in one's appreciation of music, there is always the danger of appreciating the wrong things. This is particularly true in the world of the avant-garde, where, except for one or two uniquely perceptive critics, most of us haven't a clue what's going on. You know the sort of stuff I mean; Mark Twain defined it rather well:

> **We often feel sad in the presence of music without words; and often more than that in the presence of music without music.**

Yes, the experimental can present problems to the would-be music-lover. What is strikingly original and what's just different for the sake of being different? Like this concert described in the *Western Morning News:*

> **A few will be seated in front of the quartet in approximately a conventional concert position, while the others will have more unusual relationships with the performers.**

Mind you, as I said, a gifted critic can separate the genuine from the dross. Here's a rave from the *Guardian:*

> **I was for some time uncertain about the grotesque throat-noises of the reciter-singer, Roy Hart, sounding**

as much constipated as mad, but the very embarrassment they inspired (cries of 'Rubbish' from the back)
was a designed part of a harrowing aesthetic experience
utterly new and original.

And to think we could have got that wrong and thought the cries of
'Rubbish' were just cries of 'Rubbish'! How fortunate that at most
musical performances there are notes in the programme and on the radio
there's always an announcer to clarify things. They can be very useful in
helping the listeners' recognition of individual instruments, always a hard
task in a big orchestra. Here's a letter from the BBC Director of Publicity,
published in a wartime *Daily Telegraph*:

Sir, in reply to your correspondent, Mr. Paul Nichols,
who inquires about the music which ends the BBC early
morning religious broadcasts in alternate weeks, it is
not, as he supposes, played on a concertina, but by the
BBC Symphony Orchestra.

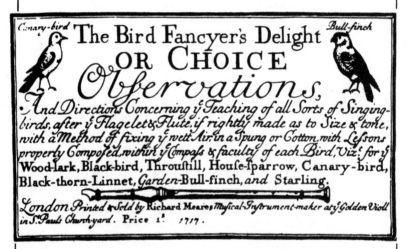

Musical instruments are beautiful artefacts and some of them have
marvellous rolling names – like Euphonium, Sousaphone, Mandolin,
Dulcimer, Marimba . . . It would be easy to get carried away just by the
sound of the words. A fact which W. S. Gilbert demonstrated in the
opening to his *Story of Prince Agib*:

Strike the concertina's melancholy string!
Blow the spirit-stirring harp like anything!
Let the piano's martial blast
Rouse the Echoes of the past,
For of Agib, Prince of Tartary, I sing!

Of Agib, who could readily, at sight,
Strum a march upon the loud Theodolite.
He would diligently play
On the Zoëtrope all day,
And blow the gay Pantechnicon all night.

For those readers who find it difficult to tell instruments apart, here's a definition of one from Ambrose Bierce:

FIDDLE, n. An instrument to tickle human ears by friction of a horse's tail on the entrails of a cat.
  To Rome said Nero: If to smoke you turn,
  I shall not cease to fiddle while you burn.
  To Nero Rome replied: Pray do your worst,
  'Tis my excuse that you were fiddling first.

While we're on definitions, let's move from instrumental to vocal music with one from Oliver Herford:

SONG – The licensed medium for bawling in public things too silly or sacred to be uttered in ordinary speech.

Singing is a very popular branch of Serious Music and the idea of taking it up professionally appeals to many young people. A report from the *Sunday Express*:

Miss April Brunner, who was deb-of-the-year in 1954 and then studied modern languages at Oxford, has decided on a new career. She wants to become a concert singer.
'I have always been interested in the stage,' she says, 'but it is such a full-time career. One would never be able to do anything else. With a concert, one would just sing for a couple of hours and then be finished.'

Here's the tale of another female vocalist, told in an anonymous limerick:

> There was a young girl in the choir
> Whose voice rose higher and higher
> Till one Sunday Night
> It rose quite out of sight
> And they found it next day on the spire.

A problem that always arises in vocal music is that of balance between the words and the music. Sometimes the marriage works perfectly, but often one or other is too dominant. Either the tune has to be kept simple so that the words can be heard clearly, or the words are sacrificed totally to the music, as, for example, in most opera. It usually is the words that take a back seat in vocal music, and this has always been the case. Aristophanes:

> For music any words are good enough.

Joseph Addison:

> Nothing is capable of being well set to music that is not nonsense.

And a rather original view of the use of words with music from Oscar Wilde:

> **If one hears bad music, it is one's duty to drown it in conversation.**

One of the most loved mixes of words and music is opera. At least it's loved by people who love it; it has also inspired a great deal of hatred over the years from those who don't. Ambrose Bierce, needless to say, had a fairly venomous opinion of it:

> **The actor apes a man – at least in shape;**
> **The opera performer apes an ape.**

He also provided this definition:

> **CHORUS, n. In opera, a band of howling dervishes who terrify the audience while the singers are taking breath.**

The operas which seem to stimulate the most violent emotions, both of idolatory and hatred, are those of Wagner. Here's the view of a fellow-composer, Rossini:

> **Wagner has beautiful moments, but awful quarter hours.**

And from Bill Nye:

> **Wagner's music is better than it sounds.**

That remark was quoted by Mark Twain, who himself had pretty strong views on the composer's work. Here he is on the subject of 'Lohengrin':

> **The banging and slamming and booming and crashing were something beyond belief. The racking and pitiless pain of it remains stored up in my memory alongside the memory of the time that I had my teeth fixed.**

Part of the difficulty with any opera is understanding what's going on. Since you can never hear the words, and they are rarely in English, it's as well to know the story or you have no idea why all these people arrive on stage and sing. Opera repays homework. Mark Twain again:

> **I have attended operas, whenever I could not help it, for fourteen years now; I am sure I know of no agony comparable to listening to an unfamiliar opera.**

Before we leave opera, here's an epigram from the early nineteenth century, when, let us remember, they loved excruciating puns:

ON BALLS AND OPERAS

> **If by their names we things should call,**
> **It surely would be properer**
> **To term a singing piece a *bawl*,**
> **A dancing piece a *hopperer*.**

Oh dear. Let's move hastily on to ballet, with another little poem, 'The Song of the Ballet' by J. B. Morton:

> **Lift her up tenderly,**
> ** Raise her with care,**
> **Catch hold of one leg,**
> ** And a handful of hair;**
> **Swing her round savagely,**
> ** And when this palls,**
> **Heave-ho! Away with her**
> ** Into the stalls.**

And, while we're with J. B. Morton, let's hear one of his musical definitions:

> **PRODIGY: A child who plays the piano when he ought to be asleep in bed.**

Nurse (to fond mother of celebrated musical prodigy).
" Please, Mum, is Master Willy to 'ave 'is morning sleep, or
go on wiv 'is Sixteenth Sympherny ? "

Mind you, if children are going to succeed in the world of Serious Music,
you've got to start young. I think I'll close this chapter with a report on a
young musician, from the *Darlington and Stockton Times:*

> **Fourteen-year-old Victor Harris has passed with credit
> two of the recent Royal Academy of Music piano
> examinations. For failing to stop he was fined £5.**

CINEMA

*"Damned thing's been following us about all day
hoping to be discovered."*

The cinema box-office girl noticed an Irishman come back for another ticket only seconds after buying one. A few moments later he was back to buy a third. 'Why do you keep buying tickets?' she asked.

'Well,' he said, 'there's a big fella inside the door who keeps tearing them up on me.'

'Why did the film-mad chicken cross the road?'

'I don't know. Why did the film-mad chicken cross the road?'

'To see Gregory Peck.'

Two little boys in Hollywood were insulting each other.

'Yah. I bet my Dad can beat your Dad.'

'Oh yeah? Your Dad *is* my Dad.'

Did you hear about the cinema usherette who left on her first night because she had seen the main feature?

Business in some cinemas is getting very bad. I rang up our local Odeon the other day and asked, 'What time's the main feature?'

The manager said, 'What time can you make it?'

A new film's just come out from behind the Iron Curtain. It's a real tear-jerker about a Russian peasant woman who's so poor she had to take in brains to wash.

One movie-star was so rich, she even had her initials monogrammed on the bags under her eyes.

An actor was offered £5,000 a week to work on a new film. 'That's amazingly good money,' he said. 'What's the movie called?'

'It's a remake of *Treasure Island*,' the director replied. 'And you're playing Long John Silver. Now I want you to be on the set first thing Tuesday morning.'

'For that kind of money,' said the actor, 'I'd be happy to start on Monday.'

'No,' said the director. 'Monday you're having your leg off.'

'Can I kiss you?' the nervous young man asked his girl on their first date in the back row of the cinema.

She didn't reply, so he asked in a louder whisper.

Still no response, so he tried again even louder.

By this time people around them were hushing him up, so he leant across to the girl's ear and said in a loud and clear voice, 'What's the matter – are you deaf?'

'No,' she replied. 'Are you paralysed?'

Did you hear about the film cameraman who had to give up his job after he had a vasectomy. He couldn't stand the way the director kept saying, 'Cut!'

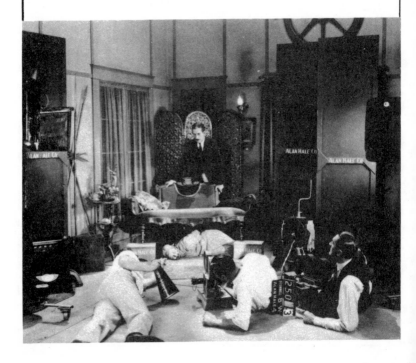

The Cinema is so much a part of our lives that it is sometimes a shock to remember how comparatively young the medium is. Within a century it has developed its techniques and artistic potential and even created its own mythology. The film industry is the great dream machine. At one end of the scale it peddles glamour and escapism to the masses; at the other it produces art-movies of such highbrow complexity that no one can understand them; and there are any number of different styles in between.

But primarily the cinema is a great commercial business. And all other considerations come second to profit. In the words of Richard Winnington:

It is the business of Hollywood to shape truth into box office contours.

And if art suffers in this shaping process, that's just part of the game. An anonymous thought on the subject:

Film rights are the blood money producers pay to authors when they are about to murder their books.

And when the book is a classic that's out of copyright, they don't even have to pay; the only complaint they get is the silent one of the author turning in his grave. And that wouldn't stop a Hollywood film producer. If the film needs more sex than the book supplied, if adding a Japanese star to a film about Julius Caesar will help the worldwide sales, if changing the hero's sex will make a good part for a star actress, then it has to happen, so that the backers make their money. And that's important, even in this country. A little verse, 'On British Films' by Basil Boothroyd:

> **Isn't it funny**
> **How they never make any money,**
> **While everyone *in* the racket**
> **Cleans up such a packet?**

But it's not just lack of money that threatens the film industry. There's also the impact of television, making its own programmes, showing old movies, even making films specially for television. And it has other advantages over the cinema. An anonymous American thought on the subject:

I like television better – it's not so far to the bathroom.

And yet somehow the film industry staggers on. There seem to be no fewer film stars today than there were in the golden days of Hollywood. The cinema was really responsible for the international star system. Before its invention there were plenty of entertainers who had great followings at their performances, but it was only when those performances could be reproduced and shown all over the world at the same time that international stardom became a reality.

And the cinema had other advantages for actors, as Will Rogers observed:

The movies are the only business were you can go out front and applaud yourself.

To be a film star has become one of the great twentieth-century dreams, but it can be a very limiting rôle. A report from the *North-Western Evening Mail:*

The public is very faithful to screen favourites, provided they remain in the type of parts expected of them. Occasionally, a comedian is permitted to try his hand at comedy or vice versa, but this sort of thing is not greatly encouraged.

A loyal public can be a nuisance to the film star, and most of them spend large amounts of their enormous payments buying privacy. Some take it a bit too far. Fred Allen:

Some movie stars wear their sunglasses even in church; they're afraid God might recognize them and ask for autographs.

The Smart Screen Magazine

SCREENLAND

May
25c

Loretta
Young

"GRAND HOTEL"
with Garbo,
the Barrymores,
Joan Crawford,
REVOLUTIONIZES
HOLLYWOOD!

Who is
the Man
Cagney
Fears?

Gay Fiction—Douglas Fairbanks, Jr.'s New Film

"There's somebody in there at the moment—when he's seen it, you can go in."

Because film stars spend so much time and effort keeping away from their public, the fans have to rely on the press for news of their idols. Papers are full of such irrelevant titbits as this from *The Star*:

> **In her next picture she will not wear any glamorous clothes. It's a story of the wide open spaces.**

Even in these days of frank chat-shows and revealing interviews, there is still a mystique which surrounds a star. Perhaps it's with good reason that the public is kept at a distance. In the words of Oscar Levant:

> **Strip away the phoney tinsel of Hollywood and you'll find the real tinsel underneath.**

It's partly because the world of films is in some respects a phoney world that it inspires a great deal of disapproval. This is obviously evident with certain notorious films which are thought unsuitable for public viewing, but for some people any film is by definition evil. News from the *Dartmouth Western Guardian:*

> **A lady in the audience reminded the meeting that the Bible told them the Kingdom of Heaven would come like a thief in the night. Suppose the Kingdom came on a Sunday night. What a terrible thing it would be for those people in the cinema.**

More information from a wartime *News Chronicle:*

> **Rhyl cinemas can only be opened on Sundays if it is wet at 2 p.m. A recent dispute about the weather has now resulted in Rhyl Council introducing a new rule. In future, the chairman of the council and the town clerk will decide if the weather is 'wet enough' for the cinemas to open.**

Part of the moral anxiety people feel about the cinema is based on what the audience gets up to when the lights go down. Some of it defies belief, if the evidence is anything to go by. From the *Sunday Chronicle:*

> **Two dentures found under a seat in a Beckenham cinema after the last performance of *Kiss in the Dark* are still unclaimed.**

In spite of what puritans may fear, the vast majority of the public go to the cinema to see films rather than to cuddle in the back row. (Indeed, many modern films offer too much competition to allow the amateur Casanova to feel at his ease.) But what is it that makes people go to the cinema? It must be the publicity, the little description in the press which tells you this is your sort of film. From a Kentish paper:

> **An amazingly gripping story of ten men lost in the dessert.**

From *What's On In London:*

> **Roaring sequences of bloody sea battles; quieter moments of love and sickness in the captain's cabin.**

And from a Nigerian newspaper:

> **A cowboy rode one way into town humming and every-one kept away from him. Another cowboy rode his horse from the other end. Both were famous for their quick drawers.**

It's all publicity and the film industry thrives on publicity. Except in a few specialised areas, where secrecy is more highly valued. A report from the *Brighton and Hove Gazette:*

> **Brighton Film Studios are making a Conservative propaganda film without a name. The public will not be allowed to see it.**

(Obviously the original Blue Movie.)

The cinema is often described as 'larger than life', and sheer size is highly respected. Lack of money has limited the number of epic productions, but the aim is still to make each film bigger and better than all that have preceded it. Beryl Pfizer:

All movies used to be 'colossal'. Now they're all 'frank'. I think I liked 'colossal' better.

For colossal movies everything must be colossal. At least as colossal as the real thing – preferably more colossal. A report from the *Daily Mail* in the 'forties:

It's well known that the British film unit which went to Egypt recently for scenes in Shaw's *Caesar and Cleopatra* took their own home-made sphinx along. (It was more photogenic.) What's less well known is that they left it there 'for Egypt'. Producer Gabriel Pascal says he got a local stonemason to engrave the plaque: 'With the compliments of J. Arthur Rank'.

Film Fun 2ᵈ

EVERY TUESDAY

No. 327. Vol. 7.   April 17th, 1926.

The Lively Larks of— HAROLD LLOYD
The Pathé Mirth Merchant
This Week: "BEATEN AT THE POST!"

1. "Now you stay there till I come back," said the lovely Laura, who was out shopping, to Harold. "Don't move from that spot!" Of course, Harold promised not to budge. But in the offing was Harold's rival, one Horatio Haggis, and he was so furious that his nice neat hair-parting went all zigzag.

2. "My girl!" he hissed, gnashing his ears with jealousy. "But I'll shift him! This'll be a very moving picture, with Harold Lloyd, Esquire, moving right out of it!" Saying which he made a noose in the rope trailing from the passing steam-roller and dropped it over the post, whilst Harold yawned.

3. On went the flint-flattener, and the portion of pavement round that post got pulled clean away, being a bit part-worn at the seams. So there was Harold, who by this time, had dropped into a doze, being taken for a joy-ride. "That's got rid of him!" cackled Horatio. "Now I can wait for Laura!"

4. But not so. For the steam-roller went right round and came back the same way again, just as Laura returned from her ribbon-matching. "Here we are, then!" chortled Harold. "I'm just where you left me!" Wasn't Horatio mad at being thus done! Oh dear, he did chat! *(Continued on page 24.)*

These outsize productions were usually mounted by outsize personalities, men who could control temperamental casts of thousands. Here's a little dialogue that is supposed to have occurred when Sam Goldwyn was watching the filming of *The Last Supper*. He summoned an underling and asked:

> **'Why only twelve?'**
> **'That's the original number.'**
> **'Well, go out and get thousands.'**

There are many other stories about Goldwyn. He originated the famous line:

> **A verbal contract isn't worth the paper it's written on.**

And, when someone admired his wife's hands, he is reputed to have said:

> **Yes, I'm going to have a bust made of them.**

People in films tend to gather such stories about them. They have to think big. A clerihew by Nicolas Bentley:

> **Cecil B. DeMille,**
> **Rather against his will,**
> **Was persuaded to leave Moses**
> **Out of the Wars of the Roses.**

The cinema is blamed for a lot of criminal activity and arguments about cause and effect continue unabated. Sometimes the relationship between screen violence and real violence is close. From the *Yorkshire Evening Press:*

> **A York man told Howden magistrates yesterday he felt**
> **'violent' after seeing the James Bond film *Thunderball*.**
> **He pleaded guilty to stealing binder twine, assaulting a**
> **policeman, destroying a pigeon cote and damaging a**
> **police raincoat.**

Yes, that sort of thing really gets people going. And it's the same with sex. That's why the censor is there – to protect people from the wicked things they might see at the cinema. From the *Evening Standard:*

> **One reason *Great Expectations* had to be classed as an**
> **'A' film was that it happened to have a bed in it.**

And while you're reeling from the shock-waves of that, I think I'll finish the chapter. We'll close with a Film Director's Epitaph:

Here I lie, a lonely creature,
Edited out of life's great feature.
My next scene (like many others before)
Has ended up on the cutting-room floor.

Fig. 10.—Butcher's Empire Camera

TELEVISION

They say television's killing the art of conversation. It's true. I went round to a friend's house the other day and found the entire family gathered round the set, gawping. The only one who spoke was the budgie. It said, 'Shut up. Sit down. It's on.'

A husband came back from work one night and found there was no food in the house. He said to his wife, 'Why didn't you go to the shops?'

She said, 'There's no point. The television's broken down so I wouldn't know what to buy,'

Do you know, I once lived in a semi-detached house with very thin walls. I didn't mind hearing the neighbours' radio all the time, but I could see their television as well.

Did you hear about the Irishman who bought a black and white dog because he thought the licence would be cheaper?

Two girls talking... One says, 'Do you prefer watching television or going out with your boyfriend?'

'Not much in it, really,' said the other. 'Either way I get a lot of interference.'

I knew a TV comic once who was so vain that every time he opened his fridge and the light came on, he took a bow.

Some late-night chat-shows are so infantile it seems criminal to keep them up so late.

The boys down at the factory called her 'Television', because she never had much on on Saturday nights, and she often gave repeat performances during the week.

Did you hear about the Irishman who went on *The Generation Game?* He won a pair of sliding doors and a conveyor belt.

I saw a really old gangster movie on the television last night. I mean really old! It was one of those in which the robbers drove up to the bank – and found a parking space directly outside!

They're making a new spin-off series in the States called *Son of The Invisible Man*. It's about a young man with serious problems. He wants to follow in his father's footsteps – but he can't find them.

A woman said, 'I used to like television, but all the violence has put me off. Every time I switch on *Crossroads*, my husband clouts me.'

"There's always something somewhere."

It's now an established fact that watching television is the most popular leisure activity in this country, far exceeding the attractions of sport or model-making or reading or anything else. The hold of the medium is so strong that it's sometimes difficult to imagine how people filled their evenings before its invention.

The effects of this massive popularity are far-reaching. Television has its influence on every aspect of life. Even health. Doctors have diagnosed a condition known as 'television tummy'. Apparently sitting and eating slumped in front of the box for hours on end has very nasty effects on the stomach muscles.

The strange thing about television is that, despite its popularity, no one has a good word to say for it. Perhaps people so much take the technological miracle for granted that they are no longer impressed, and simply feel that, if entertainment appears in their sitting-rooms, then they are entitled to criticise it savagely. Or it may be that they fear the compulsive habit of television-viewing which threatens to take over their lives. In the words of Orson Welles:

> **I hate television; I hate it as much as peanuts, and I can't stop eating peanuts.**

Others have been equally dismissive of the medium. A prophecy by C. P. Scott:

> **Television? No good will come out of this device. The word is half Greek and half Latin.**

Al Witton:

> **Television has brought mediocrity within everyone's reach.**

Fred Allen:

> **TELEVISION: A device that permits people who haven't anything to do to watch people who can't do anything.**

Frank Lloyd Wright:

TELEVISION: Chewing-gum for the eyes.

Robert Orben:

TELEVISION SET: A machine with a picture in front; tubes in the middle; and an instalment behind.

And a rather back-handed compliment from Sam Goldwyn:

Why should people go out and pay money to see bad films when they can stay at home and see bad television for nothing?

One of the reasons for the volume of criticism about television is that it is still a new medium, still developing its style and sorting out its identity. As an anonymous wit put it:

They say TV is still in its infancy, which helps to explain why you have to get up so much and change it.

E. B. White commented on the early days of the medium:

It must have been two years ago that I attended a television demonstration at which it was shown beyond reasonable doubt that a person sitting in one room could observe the nonsense in another.

The developing medium had a profound influence on the young who grew up with it. Here are the views of a notable expert, Nigel Molesworth, the misspelling schoolboy reprobate created by Geoffrey Willans and Ronald Searle:

HEE-HEE FOR TEE-VEE:
Gosh super! we hav something to contend with which no other generation hav ever had before i.e. the television cheers cheers cheers. Everybody kno wot a t.v. is it is a square box with a screen. You switch it on and o happen, then just when you hav given up hope and are going off to buzz conkers a great booming voice say 'That's an interesting point, postlethwaite. Wot does higginbottom feel? Higginbottom?' ect. ect. It may be an interesting

82

point but i could not care less and just go away agane when a ghastley face suddenly appere. It is worse than a squished tomato but it hold me in hypnotic trance and it is the same with molesworth 2, tho he always look dopey like that. We sit and watch more and more ghastley faces with our mouths open and even forget to chew the buble gum we are slaves of the machine.

After that closely-argued thesis, perhaps we should consider television as a projector of personality. It is now easily the most important medium for instant fame. At its best it does introduce the eminent to the public. Gore Vidal:

Television is now so desperately hungry for material that they're scraping the top of the barrel.

And here's a supremely arrogant remark from Noël Coward:

Time has convinced me of one thing: television is for appearing on – not for looking at.

But we mustn't forget the educational value of television. Groucho Marx:

I find television very educating. Every time someone turns on the set I go into the other room and read a book.

Education on television doesn't escape from the charge that is levelled at everything else on the box – that television trivialises in the constant search for novelty and sensation. Richard G. Stern:

Anybody can shock a baby, or a television audience. But it's too easy, and the effect is disproportionate to the effort.

'I've been offered a marvellous job with I.T.V. treating studio audiences for hysteria'

But, while it's easy to shock, it's more difficult to go on shocking, and that's what television is most commonly accused of – weakening the impact of emotion by constant exposure. That's another reason why people get so vehement in their hatred of the medium. But in some cases the motive for criticism is less worthy. It can be just snobbery, as in this letter to *The Listener:*

> **Speaking personally, I would never contemplate the notion of watching a television programme, because the idea that I might be doing exactly the same thing as 20 million other people is repulsive to me.**

Of course one should not condemn anything unseen; that is mere prejudice. One should watch television and then condemn it. Follow the example of James Thurber:

> **About once a month, after dinner, I gird up my loins such as they are, take as deep a breath as I can, throw my shoulders back as far as they will go, walk into the room with the television set, boldly turn it on, picking a channel at random, and then see how long I can stand it.**

With practice, one can apparently stand it all evening. Part of the attraction is the people, the familiar faces. It looks a glamorous life out there on the little screen. No wonder everyone wants to be a television star. Shepherd Mead:

> **If you have no talent or no special ability, if you are plain, stupid, or even a little repulsive, you need not be discouraged. Some of the people who have become richest in television are people just like *you.***

In spite of all the knocking television gets, there are things to be said in its favour. Apart from the breadth and variety of entertainment it offers, it can also serve certain social functions. Here's an extract from a letter to the *Daily Mirror:*

> **Three of my children went to approved schools for minor offences. Another was beginning to go the same way until I got a TV on the HP.**
> **The boy became as good as gold. He started to go to church after watching services on television, and would not go out even when we wanted him to. Since the set went back because of non-payments, he has reverted to his old ways.**

*"BBC1 really is moving current affairs
down-market."*

Apart from just keeping youngsters off the streets, television can play a
more positive rôle in their upbringing. Here's a suggestion from a letter
printed in *John Bull:*

> **As children seem to take notice of everything they see on
> television these days, it would set a great example to us
> all if the saying of grace before meals was incorporated
> into the food advertisements. Grace is now said in so few
> homes – and here is a chance for television to lead us
> back to the gracious age.**

And then there's the entertainment value of television, which is often a lot better than this line by Franklin P. Jones would suggest:

Poor reception is about the only way you can improve some television programmes.

Think of the range of what television offers – News, Sport, Drama, Discussion, Serials, Children's Programmes and, of course, Light Entertainment. Television invests an enormous amount of effort and money into making people laugh. Some feel that this development has been at the expense of live theatre and music hall. A famous remark from Fred Allen:

Vaudeville is dead, and television is the box they buried it in.

"Don't throw away the Radio or TV Times—they'll come in handy next year."

But the medium can rise to the big occasion with its variety shows. Think of the endless entertainment of Christmas. Here's a line from Willis Hall and Bob Monkhouse:

Christmas is a three-day festival dedicated to the birth of Bing Crosby.

(In recent years those three days seem to have spread to about a fortnight.)

Television is sometimes accused of being an upstart medium, but one must not forget that it is part of a continuing historical process. For example, if you go to Suffolk and look at the tomb of the sixteenth-century Duke of Norfolk in Framlingham Parish Church, you will discover this interesting gobbet of information about him from the guidebook.

> **[The Duke] figured prominently in the TV series *The Six Wives of Henry VIII*.**

I'm sure the Duke would be suitably honoured to know his greatest claim to fame. But television is powerful. It has far-reaching consequences, as evidenced by this report from the *Leicester Mercury*:

> **Latest victims of television – Leicester's public conveniences. So many people now stay at home at night that takings all over the city have fallen by about 12%.**

Some people do seem to be completely lost without their sets. I suppose they're terrified of having to fall back on primitive amusements like conversation. Here's a report from the *Yorkshire Evening Post*:

> **People living on the new NCB estate in the village are unable to obtain a reasonable picture on their TV sets because there is not enough electrical power in the village, the council was told.**
> **'I had to go to bed at eight recently, because I couldn't get a picture of any kind on my set,' complained Mr. Peter McDonald.**

And even sadder news from the *Daily Herald*:

> **A couple returned early from their honeymoon yesterday because the cottage where they were staying didn't have a TV set. The 21-year-old husband, John Johnstone, said: 'There was nothing at all to do but eat and sleep.'**

It must be very confusing for people with that dependence on television to encounter anyone who doesn't share it. Here's a mother's heart-rending plea from the *Daily Mirror:*

> **How can I get my two-year-old daughter interested in television? We sit her in front of the set. She watches for a minute and says, 'Switch it off, Mummy.' I should hate to think that my daughter will grow up uninterested in TV.**

And before you get uninterested in television, I will close the chapter with an Epitaph on a Television Personality by Tom St. Brien:

He died while appearing on *This Is Your Life*.
His head and a camera were in collision.
It was rather sad for the poor man's wife,
But it did make super television.

"If it's any consolation, comrade, the dramatised reconstruction of your trial came second in the British TV ratings."

RADIO

Captain Leonard Plugge, of London, England, picks up concerts wherever he travels in Europe, by means of a 9-tube loop receiver. The set's tuning controls are attached to the instrument board of the car and the loudspeaker unit is built into the roof. Thus the set is always available for use

I've got one of these new miniature Japanese radios. It's the size of a pinhead and it's got five wave-bands, VHF, stereo, cassette recorder, perfect reproduction. Only trouble is I can't find it.

A friend of mine has a little boy who's always listening to disc jockey programmes. The other night my friend was passing his son's bedroom and heard the little fellow saying his prayers. He was saying, 'God bless Mummy and Daddy, and this request also goes out to Auntie Edith who lives in Cleethorpes, Uncle Fred and Cousin Maureen, not forgetting Bonzo the dog.'

Did you hear about the disc jockey who went to see a Doctor of Music complaining of a slipped disc?

Two men were sitting waiting to have interviews for a job as a radio announcer and one said to the other, 'Have you done much of this sort of work before?'

'N-n-n-n-no,' came the reply. 'N-n-n-n-n-none, actually. Th-th-th-th-this is m-m-m-m-my f-f-f-f-first t-t-t-t-try.'

A week later they met by chance in the street and the first one asked, 'Did you get the job?'

'N-n-n-n-n-no,' said the other. 'They s-s-s-s-said I was too t-t-t-t-t-t-t-t-t-t-t-t-t-t-t-t-t-t-tall.'

There was a girl used to live down our road – we called her Radio Sal. Whatever the frequency, you were guaranteed good reception.

People are a menace with their transistor radios. Wherever you go, out in the country, on the beach, radios blaring away. It's terrible, I can hardly hear myself playing my bagpipes.

Quintophonic sound is the latest thing with radio enthusiasts. The music goes around and around, and it comes out of here, and there...and here...and there...and there...and here...

When I was young, before the invention of the transistor, I used to listen on a cat's whisker. Got a lot of interference, though — it kept purring.

An interviewer for a BBC radio programme was sent to interview a Roman Catholic priest and found that he had arrived in the church at the time confessions were being heard. He thought it would be rather a good atmospheric touch if he conducted the interview through the confessional grille. So he queued up behind all the penitents and, when his turn came, approached the grille and said, 'May I speak to you for a moment, Father? I work for the BBC.'

'My son,' said the priest, 'I am glad you have come to see me. It must take a lot of courage to make a confession like that.'

Mistress (pointing out cobweb) "HAVEN'T YOU SEEN THIS"
New Help. "LOR, YES. SOMEFINK TO DO WITH YER WIRELESS. AIN'T IT?"

The development of radio put an end to the idea of silence. With its invention everyone had the opportunity to surround themselves by instant noise. In the words of Giraud Chester and Garnet R. Garrison:

Through the medium of broadcasting, we have been conditioned to a steady stream of words and music during our working day; radio provides a background for our study, conversation, cooking, eating, travelling, and even our thinking.

That's progress. Here's Will Rogers on the subject:

Course, we don't get meat as often as our forefathers, but we have our peanut butter and radio.

A definition from Peter Lind Hayes:

Radio is the manly art of shouting brave words into a defenceless microphone.

Others have read more into the relationship between broadcaster and public. Here's the view of Michael Kustow, published in the *Radio Times:*

Let us come to the next flashpoint. Sex. I'd like to put the proposition to you that being a single person in a room with a radio set is like being in bed with someone. It's essentially an erotic situation.

One of the problems of listening to the radio is the purely technical one of hearing. Though technology has improved enormously, you can still get a rather gravel-path sort of reception out of a cheap transistor. And some better radio sets are distinctly temperamental. Here's James Thurber on the subject:

I have never had a portable radio that worked very well for me. I say 'for me' because other people can often

make my radio go when I can't. I have what some of my friends call a 'dead thumb'. When I apply it to the knob of a radio set, there is a curious mechanical resistance. The box either goes completely dead, or gives a high whiny sound, like 'squee-ee-een' or says 'thog, thog, thog', and stops. Now and then I get a few bars of disconsolate banjo music, from some imaginary station, but that's all. One smart-looking portable I bought in Hollywood ten years ago played all right for a week and then began to go 'spreet' and 'awp awp' when I clicked the knob. I found out, after wrestling with it, that it would work properly on its back on the floor. That is, it worked properly on its back for a week. Then it would only go if it were set on something higher than my head. Such a place is hard to find in the average, or normal house. A housewife objects to a radio that has to be set on the mantelpiece, or hung from the ceiling, or placed on a

ULTRA-MODERN RECEPTION

step half-way up the front stairs. In the end the thing would only play if I held it in my hand. This is an uncomfortable way to listen to a concert or a ball game. Your wrist gets numb.

In Radio the broadcaster does his best to talk directly to his audience, and this one-to-one relationship means that listeners get very interested in the lives of the presenters they hear. You may remember the old song about Little Betty Bouncer, who loved an announcer down at the BBC. The interest doesn't always go that far, but, particularly before the advent of television, it used to be pretty strong. So much so that programmes could be fed by it. Here's a report from a wartime *Sunday Express:*

A BBC announcer will stand on his head reading a news bulletin in the Home Service Programme on March 8 and on March 10 for the Forces. This is part of the puzzle corner prize competition, and listeners will be asked to guess which of three announcers he is.

Announcers and newsreaders have other problems, apart from their personal following. Jack de Manio:

So used have people become over the forty-five years of broadcasting to hearing the news bulletins read with the same irreproachable gravity and always on the dot, that a failure seems far more rare than a breakdown of Big Ben. Now I do not know what goes on inside Big Ben, but if it is anything like what sometimes happens to newsreaders I am astonished the clock ever works at all.

Nowadays personality cults in radio centre on disc jockeys rather than announcers and newsreaders. So much airtime is taken up with popular music and so many people listen to it that this is hardly surprising. Here's Harry V. Wade's view of the essential qualities for a disc jockey:

The ideal voice for Radio may be defined as having no substance, no sex, no owner, and a message of importance to every housewife.

In that sort of broadcasting, content is not important. Fred Allen:

Sense doesn't make sense in radio.

For your wireless

For your gramophone

Beautiful to look at

As an heirloom

THE WIRELESS TABLE

A handsome solid oak piece of furniture that houses your wireless and adds beauty to your home. 28 inches high. Twist legs. Cabinet for accumulators, etc. CARRIAGE & PACKING 1/6 EXTRA **£2. 7s. 6d.**

PETER JONES LTD.
SLOANE SQUARE, S.W.1

Though disc jockeys gather huge numbers of fans, those who dislike them are equally fanatical. There's the music they play, for a start. An anonymous quip:

> **Every time we hear a disc jockey play the top 40 tunes, we get the shakes thinking what the bottom 40 must sound like.**

And for some the eternal bonhomie of the disc jockeys themselves can be a little depressing. Here's an anguished address to one from Wilson Mizner:

> **If you don't get off the air, I'll stop breathing it.**

THE FIRST BROADCAST OF BIG BEN, FROM A NEIGHBOURING ROOF
(*Shortly afterwards the microphone was fixed inside the clock tower itself*)

But disc jockeys are company and the company element is an important part of radio's success. Listening to the same programme as a lot of other people can give a sense of community. In the early days listeners really entered into the spirit of the thing. Here's part of a letter published in the *Sunday Chronicle* in the 'forties:

> **I wonder how many answer the BBC speaker's hearty 'Good morning to you all'? I do. I say, 'Good morning to you, and to dear old home, and to my beloved King and Queen.'**

Taking radio so personally can lead to problems, though. News from the *Daily Mail* in the 'fifties:

> **Miss Blank, 28-year-old domestic servant, threw a brick through a window in Broadcasting House, and told the police: 'I felt the BBC wanted livening up a bit. We have been having some lousy programmes lately.'**

That could open up a whole new field of Audience Research – counting the broken windows in Broadcasting House.

In commercial radio Audience Research becomes Market Research. Though a comparatively new development in this country, commercial radio has a long history in America, where the control of the sponsors is often total. Here's an historical analogy of how it started, from Llewellyn White:

> **Like the beleaguered Czechs of ancient Bohemia, the broadcasters had cried out for succour. Like the Hapsburgs, the advertising men who came to rescue remained to rule. And like many a philosophical Slav, the broadcasters accepted the conqueror's tongue.**

The conqueror's tongue was frequently the inanities of advertising jingles. But for the sponsors, it didn't matter what people thought of these, so long as they listened. Here's some advice from Charles Hull Wolfe's *Modern Radio Advertising:*

> **Make your announcement either intensely liked or intensely disliked. It does not matter if people repeat your commercial in slightly derisive mimicry.**

In the old days advertisements used to be read out live by the presenters, and this practice from time to time led to unfortunate misreadings. Here are a couple. First, for a famous footcare specialist:

If you think *your* feet are bad, you should see Dr. Scholl's.

And one for the soft drink 7-UP:

Remember the name – it's a big Seven and U – P after.

Anyone who works in radio knows how easy it is to make mistakes. It's hard enough to keep the words in the right order when reading from a script, but in ad lib speaking the opportunities for error are even greater. So if ever you laugh at an announcer's gaffe, spare a thought for the poor fellow and try to imagine how you'd do in his place.

The trouble with broadcast errors is that, unless you've actually heard them, you can't be sure whether they're genuine or whether they're the product of 'Wouldn't it be terrible if . . .' conversations. But here are a few that are supposed to have happened. First, from a very new announcer:

It is ten o'clock Greenwich. Meantime here is the news.

From a weather forecast:

**And tonight Northern areas can expect incest and rain –
I'm sorry, incessant rain.**

RADIO CONCERT IN THE FIELDS AT THE «AMOVETS» STATE FARM

From a cricket commentary:

> **Here's Miller running in to bowl. He's got two short legs and one behind.**

From another sports reporter:

> **And now over for hearse racing at Horst Park.**

There are plenty more around in the mythology of radio, but unfortunately the best ones are unprintable. But here's a little something which is reputed to have been printed in the *Radio Times:*

9-30 THE LIFE OF HORATIO NELSON
(For details see top of column)

It's a strange fact, but true, that the public expect much higher moral standards from Radio than Television. Perhaps it's because it's the older medium; it is expected to stand up for good old-fashioned values, and people are shocked when they detect any falling-short in broadcast material.

The treatment of Royalty is a particularly sensitive area. A report from the *News Chronicle* in the 'forties:

> **Colonel ——, the publisher, heard last night's 'Twenty Questions' and later said he was so disgusted with an 'object' chosen – Queen Mary's umbrella – that he was returning an order for books sent to his firm by the BBC.**

And here's a letter published more recently in the *Yorkshire Post:*

> **Most people are pained and ashamed when they hear news about strikes, etc., announced before news about the Royal Family. I would ask all loyal people to send a postcard to the BBC urging them to put Royal news in its proper place.**

The broadcasting of drama can also lead to embarrassment. A letter sent to the *News Chronicle:*

> **My wife and I are not prudes, but we avoid each other's eyes and switch off in nine cases out of ten when plays are being broadcast.**

And when religion's on the radio, you're dealing with dynamite. Thank goodness that most listeners at least retain a proper respect for that. A letter from *Reveille:*

> **My goldfish is religious. He stays still as a stone, in a reverent attitude, while the service is on the radio on Sundays. Then, when *Family Favourites* comes on, he darts about gaily.**

I'll end this chapter with an 'Epitaph on a Disc Jockey', by Osbert Mint:

> **Now death has come and death has done**
> **What many wished they could.**
> **He had a request from everyone**
> **To switch me off for good.**

POETRY

Amateur " Minimus Poet " (*who has called at the office twice a week for three months*). " Could you use a little poem ot mine?" *Editor* (*ruthlessly determined that this shall be his final visit*). " Oh, I think so. There are two or three broken panes of glass, and a hole in the skylight. How large is it?"

A Regimental Sergeant Major was bawling out his squad. 'Right, there's a new training programme starting tomorrow on culture. Got that? And the first item on the course is a lecture on Keats. Keats! I bet most of you horrible lot don't even know what a Keat is!'

'Ah, I met this girl once brought out all the poetry in me. She had lips like petals.'
   'Bicycle petals.'
   'And ears like flowers.'
   'Cauliflowers.'
   'No, no, her ears were like shells.'
   'Howitzer shells.'
   'She had skin like a peach.'
   'All rough and hairy.'
   'And teeth like stars.'
   'They came out at night.'

There was a young man of Japan
Whose poetry never would scan;
   When they said it was so,
   He replied, 'Yes, I know,
But I always try to get as many words into the last line as ever I possibly can.'

Milton wrote *Paradise Lost*. Then his wife died and he wrote *Paradise Regained*.

'Which poet had his head in the gallery and his feet in the stalls?'
   'Longfellow.'

'Which poet wrote all his poems in the synagogue?'
   'Rabbi Burns.'

'What are you suffering from if you don't like poetry?'
   'Gray's Allergy.'

You know, Keats was so used to receiving bills when he was young that, after he'd written 'Ode to a Nightingale' and 'Ode to Melancholy', he wrote 'Owed to the Butcher', 'Owed to the Baker' and 'This Is A Final Demand'.

Three dogs died and went to Heaven, but St. Peter stopped them at the Pearly Gates and wouldn't allow them in.

'Why not?' they asked.

'Well, you see,' the saint explained, 'you're animals and you don't have souls.'

'What are souls?' they asked.

'Well,' he replied, 'human beings have souls and that means they're capable of great works of art and literature.'

'Oh, that's all right,' said the animals. 'We write music and poetry.'

'Do you? Who are you?'

'I'm Bach, that's Offenbach, and he writes doggerel.'

Poetry is the most extreme of the arts. At its best it gives sublime insights into life, at its worst it's pretentious and ridiculous. And like a shadow haunting Poetry is Verse. Some Verse never pretends to be more than that, but some Poetry doesn't quite make it, and that's Verse too.

Poetic qualities are not easily defined. Some authorities feel that they are the exclusive prerogative of the young. Robert Graves:

Most poets are dead by their late twenties.

Certainly that was true of the skills of Wordsworth, who defined the medium thus:

Poetry is the spontaneous overflow of powerful feelings; it takes its origin from emotion recollected in tranquillity.

It was defined more prosaically by Carl Sandburg:

Poetry is the synthesis of hyacinths and biscuits.

And by Gwyn Thomas:

Poetry is trouble dunked in tears.

Here's an even more basic view from George Cabanis:

Poetry and religion are the product of the smaller intestines.

The insight of poetry is summed up in a superb image by Mark Twain:

Prose wanders around with a lantern and laboriously schedules and verifies the details and particulars of a valley and its frame of crags and peaks, then Poetry comes, and lays bare the whole landscape with a single splendid flash.

And here's another equally striking definition from Don Marquis:

Poetry is what Milton saw when he went blind.

Poetry-enthusiasts should be well-read and keep up with the latest trends in the medium. But if they can't be bothered to, there's always the perfect let-out, expressed in this little poem, 'Take Heart, Illiterates' by Justin Richardson:

For years a secret shame destroyed my peace—
I'd not read Eliot, Auden or MacNiece.
But now I think a thought that brings me hope:
Neither had Chaucer, Shakespeare, Milton, Pope.

Perhaps one should take that message to heart, and start with a grounding in the classics before tackling any modern stuff. But one must bear in mind that poems which are classics now were modern when they were first written, and were criticised as such. This is how Theodore Hook greeted one great poetic milestone:

Shelley styles his new poem 'Prometheus Unbound',
And 'tis like to remain so while time circles round;
For surely an age would be spent in the finding
A reader so weak as to pay for the binding!

And in 1815, when Sir Walter Scott published his 'Field of Waterloo', it elicited this reponse from Thomas, Lord Erskine:

On Waterloo's ensanguined plain
Lie tens of thousands of the slain:
But none by sabre or by shot
Fell half so flat as Walter Scott.

Certainly that poem seems to have dropped out of the limelight; it's not one of those that's constantly being anthologised or fragmented in books of quotations. Verse does get quoted rather a lot and the result is that lines which were originally excellent become clichés by repetition. Some years ago there was a *New Statesman* competition, which aimed to get round this problem by adding an unexpected line to a much-quoted one. Here's H. A. C. Evans's improvement of W. B. Yeats:

When you are old and grey and full of sleep,
You haven't got to bother counting sheep.

Mary Demetriades tinkering with Oliver Goldsmith:

When lovely woman stoops to folly
The evening can be awfully jolly.

And June Mercer Langfield reworking a famous line by Shakespeare:

Full fathom five thy father lies,
His aqualung was the wrong size.

She. "And are all these lovely things about which you write imaginary?" *The Poet.* "Oh, no, Miss Ethel. I have only to open my eyes and I see something beautiful before me." *She.* "Oh, how I wish I could say the same!"

Poets can write about anything; traditionally, though, their work is romantic and even risqué. It's part of that hoary old myth about artists creating their own standards. Here's a report from the *West Lancashire Evening Gazette:*

On oath, Mrs. —— told the court she was sorry for
having sent such a letter. She said she was a poet of no
mean order and she believed it was a privilege of genius
to be a little indecent.

Poetic temperament is supposed to excuse a great deal of difficult behaviour, but it doesn't necessarily make poets easy to live with. Like prophets, they are often without honour in their own country. In the words of Max Eastman:

A poet in history is divine, but a poet in the next room is a joke.

But that doesn't daunt the poet in the next room. Housewife poets can find poetry in everything. News from the *Hants and Sussex Gazette:*

A visit to a Reading biscuit factory by members of Steep Women's Institute inspired Miss —— to write a poem which will be sent to the factory as a mark of appreciation.

THE DISTREST POET.

Another basic fact about all poets is that they're poor. In the eighteenth century the aspiring versifier would find a patron to support him and spend the rest of his days writing his patron's praises; nowadays poets are reduced to writing in praise of the Arts Council. There's not a lot of money in the poetry game. Addison Mizner:

Poets are born, not paid.

Albert Ellsworth Thomas:

It takes a major operation to extract money from a minor poet.

One way that a poet can make money is by turning his talent to the commercial world and writing advertising copy. This has been a possible outlet for some years. In fact, Lord Byron was once accused of receiving £600 a year for writing verses in praise of Warren's Shoe Blacking. When challenged, he would not confirm or deny the charge, so it's quite possible that he was responsible for this commercial break, which was published in *Bell's Life* in 1835:

> **'Friend,' said Aminadab to Obadiah,**
> **'Why such amazement do thy features show?'**
> **'To see, Aminadab, thy Boots on fire,**
> **And thou stand harmless in the burning glow!'**
> **'Ah! Friend, dost thou so of discernment lack–**
> **Art thou so far to common knowledge barren,**
> **Not to perceive 'tis but the radiant black**
> **That's manufactur'd by Friend Robert Warren?'**

Because the emotional stakes in poetry are so high, because it aims at such perfection of expression, it is inevitable that the failure rate is also high. English literature is full of attacks on bad poets. Alexander Pope:

> **Pensive poets painful vigils keep,**
> **Sleepless themselves to give their readers sleep.**

Samuel Taylor Coleridge – 'On a Bad Poem':

> **Your poem must eternal be, –**
> **Dear Sir, it cannot fail;**
> **For 'tis incomprehensible,**
> **And wants both head and tale.**

The obscurity of some poetry brings to mind James I's perplexed remark on the works of John Donne:

> **Dr. Donne's verses are like the peace of God; they pass**
> **all understanding.**

And here's an offensive epigram by Matthew Prior:

> **Sir, I admit your general rule,**
> **That every poet is a fool;**
> **But you yourself may serve to show it**
> **That every fool is not a poet.**

Many such strictures on bad poetry are quite justified; there's a lot of it about. Apart from the example of William MacGonagall, perhaps the greatest bad poet, there has also been some pretty mediocre stuff churned out by even the giants of English literature. In 1930 D. B. Wyndham Lewis and Charles Lee published an anthology of bad verse called *The Stuffed Owl* and to their researches I owe the following examples. First, from William Cowper:

> **The management of tyros of eighteen**
> **Is difficult, their punishment obscene.**

From Leigh Hunt:

> **The two divinest things that man has got,**
> **A lovely woman in a rural spot.**

William Nathan Stedman:

> **And when upon your dainty breast I lay**
> **My wearied head, more soft than eiderdown.**

Our Amateur Romeo (who has taken a cottage in the country, so as to be able to study without interruption). " Arise, fair sun, and kill the envious moon——" *Owner of rubicund countenance (popping head over the hedge).* " Beg pardon, zur. Be you a talkin' to Oi, zur ? "

Religious fervour can lead to dubious poetry, as some nameless writers of hymns proved. Here's an example:

Earth from afar has heard Thy fame,
And worms have learnt to lisp Thy name.

In many other cases the names of the authors of these deathless lines have not come down to us. For example, this 'Funeral Elegie upon the Death of George Sonds, Esq.', written in 1658, is anonymous:

> **Reach me a Handcerchiff, Another yet,**
> **And yet another, for the last is wett.**

Nor do we know the name of the young Tradesman Poet responsible for this love lyric:

> **No more will I endure Love's pleasing pain,**
> **Nor round my heart's leg tie his galling chain.**

This Housemaid Poet is also, regrettably, anonymous:

> **O Moon, when I gaze on thy beautiful face,**
> **Careering along through the boundaries of space,**
> **The thought has often come into my mind**
> **If I ever shall see thy glorious behind.**

One thing that all those examples demonstrate is that the writing of poetry is a highly skilled craft, not just a hobby for the enthusiastic amateur. There are all the problems of metre and rhythm. When does a poem need to rhyme and when doesn't it? This anonymous limerick evades the issue:

> **There was an old man of Dunoon**
> **Who always ate soup with a fork,**
> >   **For he said, 'As I eat**
> >   **Neither fish, fowl, nor flesh,**
> **I should otherwise finish too quick.'**

There have been many experiments with different kinds of rhyme, but some authorities think any kind of rhyme is demeaning and prefer the majesty of blank verse. Here's part of a joky experiment by Thomas Hood, which tries to get the best of both worlds:

> **Anon Night comes, and with her wings brings things**
> **Such as, with his poetic tongue, Young sung;**
> **The gas up-blazes with its bright white light,**
> **And paralytic watchmen prowl, howl, growl,**
> **About the streets to take up Pall-Mall Sal,**
> **Who, hasting to her nightly jobs, robs fobs.**
> **Now thieves, to enter for your cash, smash, crash,**

Kindly Hostess (to nervous reciter who has broken down in " The Charge of the Light Brigade "). " Never mind, Mr. Tompkins, just tell us it in your own words."

**Past drowsy Charley, in a deep sleep, creep,
But, frightened by Policeman B.3, flee
And while they're going, whisper low, 'No go.'**

Some poets just ignore all restrictions of metre and rhyme and write free verse. Robert Frost disapproved of this:

Writing free verse is like playing tennis with the net down.

But maybe the best way to simplify poetry is just to have shorter poems. Here's Justin Richardson's abbreviated version of a famous anthology piece by Thomas Gray:

**Elegy W.I. A Country Churchyard by T.G.
The curfew t's the k. of parting day.
The village elders in the churchyard plot
Might have been famous men like (e.g.) Gray;
But famous people also die. So what?**

The trouble with that poem is that it would be pretty difficult to recite, and live poetry readings are a popular source of entertainment with an enthusiastic minority. They tend to see a fairly muted show. Modern poets mostly mumble and slouch at their reading and don't run the risks

of the man reading 'The Charge of the Light Brigade' in this limerick by
Ambrose Bierce:

> There was a young reader who thundered
> And lightened, and 'rode the Six Hundred!'
>   But he got no applause
>   For his effort, because
> His trowsers it sadly had sundered.

That wouldn't happen nowadays. Modern poets are very distrustful of
over-dramatic reading. But then modern poets always have been a
strange bunch. Lord Dunsany:

> **Modern poets are bells of lead. They should tinkle
> melodiously, but usually they just klunk.**

That sort of criticism seems to be the fate of the poet. Let's continue the
melancholy strain and end the chapter with a valedictory verse by
Anthony Brode:

> **Critics sipping cups of tea
>   Praise, between their crumpets,
> Drunken poets – men who cried
>   Ha, ha among the strumpets:
> It's sad kind words are seldom said
> Until a rake is safely dead.**

CONVERSATION

'Ah, Lionel, you know it's no fun getting old. Nearly all our friends are dead now. Mind you, William Green's the one I miss most.'

'Why's that, Cecil?'

'Because I married his widow.'

'Drink makes you look extraordinarily beautiful and sexy.'

'But I haven't been drinking!'

'No, but I have.'

A railway porter told a man off for smoking in the station waiting room. 'Don't you see that notice on the wall – NO SMOKING ALLOWED?'

'Yes, I do,' said the man, 'but I can't keep all your rules. There's a notice on this wall saying WEAR LAMINATED CORSETS.'

Jones jumped up from the card table, white with rage. 'Stop the game!' he yelled. 'Smith is cheating!'

'How do you know?'

'He's not playing the hand I dealt him.'

A patient was talking to his psychiatrist. 'My wife is terrified because I smoke in bed.'

'I don't see why she should be terrified by it,' said the psychiatrist, 'but I do agree that smoking tobacco is a dangerous habit.'

'Who mentioned tobacco?'

The elephant looked down at the tiny mouse by its foot. 'Ho ho,' he said. 'You're very tiny.'

'Yes,' agreed the mouse. 'I haven't been well lately.'

'It's my husband, doctor. He's convinced he's a chicken.'

'Good heavens, madam! Why on earth didn't you tell me about this sooner?'

'Well, I would've, but we needed the eggs.'

Conversationalist. "Do you play ping-pong?"
Actor. "No. I play *Hamlet*!"

One crook was discussing getaway cars with another. 'Why do you paint yours green on one side and yellow on the other?'

'Because I like to hear the witnesses contradict each other.'

'Do you believe in God?' one goldfish asked another.
'Of course. Who do you think changes our water?'

'Tell me, Mr. O'Flaherty, how can you tell your twins apart?'
'Well, if I put my finger in Sean's mouth and he bites me, then I know it's his brother Pat.'

'Halt! Who goes there?'

'Medical Officer.'

'Halt! Who goes there?'

'I just told you. The Medical Officer.'

'Halt! Who goes there?'

'Look, what's the matter with you, man? Are you deaf or stupid or just plain insolent?'

'I'm sorry, sir. Sergeant said if anyone I didn't recognise came up to the post, I was to shout "Halt! Who goes there?" three times, and then fire.'

In a Trappist monastery there was a rule that only one monk could speak every five years, and this was explained to a young novice when he joined the order. The next morning at breakfast one of the monks said, 'I think the porridge is too sweet.'

Five years passed and it was another monk's turn. He said: 'I don't think the porridge is sweet enough.'

Another five years passed, and it was the novice's turn to speak. He said: 'I'm going. I've heard nothing but arguments since I got here.'

" Well, and what can you talk about?"

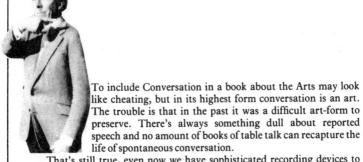

To include Conversation in a book about the Arts may look like cheating, but in its highest form conversation is an art. The trouble is that in the past it was a difficult art-form to preserve. There's always something dull about reported speech and no amount of books of table talk can recapture the life of spontaneous conversation.

That's still true, even now we have sophisticated recording devices to preserve conversation. At its best it remains a live art, and ideally a participant one. Its value has long been recognised. Let's go right back to Cicero:

> **I am very thankful to old age, which has increased my eager desire for conversation.**

The Rev. Sydney Smith:

> **One of the greatest pleasures of life is conversation.**

There's an old proverb that sums up its benefits:

> **Education begins a gentleman; conversation completes him.**

John Mason Brown:

> **A good conversationalist is not one who remembers what was said, but says what someone wants to remember.**

But conversation is not without drawbacks. Here's a characteristically cynical definition by Ambrose Bierce:

> **CONVERSATION, n. A fair for the display of the minor mental commodities, each exhibitor being too intent upon the arrangement of his own wares to observe those of his neighbour.**

A complaint from Don Herold:

Conversation is the slowest form of human communication.

And an anonymous quip on the subject:

Conversation is a form of communication in which some men never stop to think and some women never think to stop.

Conversation is not just another word for talking. It's an interchange of ideas, something created mutually by the participants. George Bernard Shaw made the distinction rather well:

The trouble with her is that she lacks the power of conversation but not the power of speech.

With conversation, as with the other arts, taste varies. H. L. Mencken:

Women have simple tastes. They can get pleasure out of the conversation of children in arms and men in love.

But, in spite of such willing listeners, everyone should try to improve his powers of conversation. By extending vocabulary, for instance. Here's a report from the *Gloucestershire Echo:*

We come from a village where we have little children who swear like troopers, without knowing the meaning of what they are saying. Can we not do something about it ourselves by putting in a word here or there when the opportunity arises?

For the novice conversationalist there are books available with advice on how to dazzle your friends and be a hit at dinner parties. There are also books of useful phrases, jokes and anecdotes which guarantee to make you socially indispensible. But beware. In the words of Jean de la Bruyère:

One of the signs of mediocrity of mind is the habit of always telling stories.

Much more important than preparing set-pieces is being prepared to follow the flow of conversation. But following the flow does not necessarily mean agreeing with everything everyone says. Benjamin Disraeli:

> **If every man were straightforward in his opinions, there would be no conversation.**

Mark Twain:

> ***Agreeing*** **with a person cripples controversy and ought not to be allowed.**

JUDY—HER JOKE.

What ! the Number wouldn't be complete without a picture of an old-fashioned Christmas party, and the happy family met together round the festive board ! Well, here you have the happy family having a few words before dinner.—It 's horribly like real life, isn't it ?

One piece of advice that is always given to the would-be conversationalist is that he should weigh and consider what he is about to say. But not for too long. Francis Rodman:

Think twice before you speak – and you'll find everyone talking about something else.

But some forethought is essential. An epigram by Matthew Prior:

They never taste who always drink,
They always talk, who never think.

There was once a girls' school headmistress who used to tell her charges to ask themselves three questions before they said anything:

Is it true?
Is it kind?
Is it necessary?

That seems a recipe for the total destruction of conversation, but maybe it's a step in the right direction. The most important question really is, have you got anything worth saying? An epigram from Richard Garnett:

I hardly ever ope my lips, one cries,
Simonides, what think you of my rule?
If you're a fool, I think you're very wise:
If you are wise, I think you are a fool.

Conversation aspires to wit; that, I suppose, is the goal, but it is not often achieved. Alexander Pope:

You beat your pate, and fancy wit will come:
Knock as you please, there's nobody at home.

Jean de la Bruyère:

It is a great misfortune neither to have enough wit to talk well, nor enough judgement to be silent.

Jonathan Swift:

There are few wild beasts more to be dreaded than a talking man having nothing to say.

And here's an epigram written by John Heywood in the sixteenth century – 'On Tongue Versus Wit':

> **Thou hast a swift running tongue: how be it,**
> **Thy tongue is nothing so quick as thy wit.**
> **Thou art, when wit and tongue in running contend,**
> **At thy wit's end ere thou be at thy tale's end.**

He.   "What a pretty fan!"
She.   "Yes; I had it given to me when I first came out!"
He.   "Really! It *has* worn well!"

Another quality of wit is that it must be original; second-hand remarks just don't count. A little verse by Justin Richardson on a supposed wit:

His epigrams are not his own –
The man's an epigramophone.

Not only is borrowing wit a rather shabby form of plagiarism, it's also to be deplored for social reasons. Or at least it was when Lord Chesterfield was advising his son on the ways of society:

A man of fashion never has recourse to proverbs and
vulgar aphorisms.

And another tip from the same source:

False English, bad pronunciation, old sayings and
common proverbs; which are so many proofs of having
kept bad and low company.

Conversation is only the surface of thought, and often what one says is some way removed from what one actually thinks. This is particularly true in a social context, where a polite exterior must be maintained at all costs. The following poem shows this process in action:

DOMESTIC ASIDES; or, TRUTH IN PARENTHESES

by Thomas Hood

'I really take it very kind,
This visit, Mrs. Skinner!
I have not seen you such an age –
(The wretch has come to dinner!)

'Your daughters, too, what loves of girls –
What heads for painters' easels!
Come here and kiss the infant, dears, –
(And give it p'rhaps the measles!)

'Your charming boys I see are home
From Reverend Mr. Russel's;
'Twas very kind to bring them both, –
(What boots for my new Brussels!)

'What! little Clara left at home?
Well now I call that shabby:
I should have lov'd to kiss her so, –
(A flabby, dabby, babby!)

'And Mr. S., I hope he's well,
Ah! though he lives so handy,
He never now drops in to sup, –
(The better for our brandy!)

'Come, take a seat – I long to hear
About Matilda's marriage;
You're come of course to spend the day! –
(Thank Heaven I hear the carriage!)

'What, must you go? next time I hope
You'll give me longer measure;
Nay – I shall see you down the stairs –
(With most uncommon pleasure!)

'Good bye! good bye! remember all,
Next time you'll take your dinners!
(Now, David, mind I'm not at home
In future to the Skinners!).'

I suppose the worst thing to be in conversation is a bore, but it's an accusation that has been levelled at some very eminent men, particularly those given to pontificating. Here's the Reverend Sydney Smith on Macaulay:

He is like a book in breeches.

Or again:

He has occasional flashes of silence, that make his conversation perfectly delightful.

Here's Dr. Johnson on one unfortunate conversationalist:

He talks like a watch which ticks away minutes, but never strikes the hour.

Deaf Old Gentleman. "The conversation seems very amusing, my dear. What is it all about ?
Hostess (fortissimo). "When they say anything worth repeating, grandpapa, *I'll tell you !* "

And on Oliver Goldsmith:

> **The misfortune of Goldsmith in conversation is this: he goes on without knowing how to get off.**

Let's give Goldsmith the right of reply; here's his view of Johnson's conversation:

> **There is no arguing with Johnson; for if his pistol misses fire, he knocks you down with the butt end of it.**

One of the chief causes of boring talking is the participant's not listening. If the talker is only thinking of himself, you don't get the give and take of true conversation. Ed Howe:

> **No man would listen to you talk if he didn't know it was his turn next.**

Joyce Cary:

> **He is an artist, you know, and talks a great deal for his own pleasure.**

And a little poem by H. A. C. Evans, entitled 'The Egoist':

> **Himself is all he'll talk about to you,**
> **A subject that, for him, has never cloyed,**
> **Thus furnishing an unimpeded view**
> **Into a vast, reverberating void.**

Some people's conversation is mesmeric and relentless; they just never stop. Sydney Smith used to judge talk on a scale like horse-power, called parson-power; he'd speak of a 'Twelve parson-power conversation'. But all of us have come across talkers who won't stop. Mark Twain knew one:

> **His tongue is in constant motion from eleven in the fore-noon till four in the afternoon, and why it does not wear out is the affair of Providence, not mine.**

Here's an anonymous eighteenth-century epigram – 'On A Great Talker':

> **To hear Dash by the hour blunder forth his vile prose,**
> **Job himself scarcely patience could keep;**
> **He's so dull that each moment we're ready to doze,**
> **Yet so noisy, we can't go to sleep.**

Let's close the chapter with a hint from Ralph Waldo Emerson, of great benefit to those who find talking a problem:

> **A man of no conversation should smoke.**

CRITICISM

TURNING A PHRASE. — *Dramatic Author.* "What the deuce do you mean by pitching into my piece in this brutal manner? It's shameful!" *Dramatic Critic.* "Pitching into it? No, no, no, dear old man—you'll see how pleased I was, *if you'll only read between the lines !*"

'How did your latest play go?'
   'Well, it got mixed notices.'
   'Mixed?'
   'Yes. We liked it, but the critics didn't.'

Three muggers criticised their Irish victim for putting up such a fierce fight when they attacked him. All they got was the small change in his pocket. 'Why did you struggle so hard for 7p?' they asked.
   'Well, I wasn't to know,' he replied. 'I thought you were after the ten pound note in my sock.'

A defendant was criticised for committing bigamy by the magistrate, who said he would give the maximum penalty. The counsel for the defence said the man had already got it – two mothers-in-law.

'I don't like the colour of your cow.'
   'It's a Jersey.'
   'Is it? I thought it was its skin.'

After attending four different plays at the Edinburgh Festival, a critic wrote, 'These four works in different national styles bring me to the following conclusion: An Englishman thinks and speaks, a Scot thinks twice before he speaks, a Welshman speaks before he thinks, and an Irishman speaks.'

A man was criticising the food in a restaurant. Holding up a piece of meat to the waitress for inspection, he asked: 'Do you call that pig?'
   'Which end of the fork?' she replied.

A greyhound owner was talking to the trainer about his dog after it had lost its fiftieth race. 'I'm going to throw him in the canal,' he said.
   'Don't waste your time,' advised the trainer. 'Just walk away from him.'

A woman bought her husband two ties for his birthday, so, dutifully, he put one of them on and went down to breakfast. When he entered the kitchen, his wife stormed at him, 'That's typical of you – you never like the presents I buy.'

'Of course I do,' he pleaded.

'Well, what's wrong with the other tie then?'

'Waiter, waiter, you've just put your thumb in my soup.'

'Not to worry, sir. It's not very hot.'

'Waiter, waiter, this coffee tastes like mud.'

''Course it does. It was ground only half an hour ago.'

'Waiter, waiter, I've been sitting here half an hour waiting to give my order.'

'I'm so sorry, sir, what would you like?'

'Half a dozen snails.'

'Fine, sir. I'll bring them right away.'

'No, let them walk. It'll be quicker.'

'Waiter, waiter, this egg isn't fresh.'

'Don't look at me, sir. I only laid the table.'

Three tortoises were in a pub and they realised that they hadn't got any cigarettes. One rather grudgingly agreed to go to the machine round the corner and get some. After three hours the remaining two were getting a bit tired of waiting and one said, 'Blimey, what's keeping him?'

The pub door opened and the third tortoise said, 'Look, if you're going to start criticising, you can get them yourself.'

Nobody likes being criticised, and so on the whole critics of the various arts have had a pretty bad press over the years. Since almost every artist has at some stage had a bad review somewhere, they tend to get very vehement on the subject of critics in general. Here's Lord Byron on the subject:

> **As soon**
> **Seek roses in December, ice in June;**
> **Hope constancy in wind, or corn in chaff;**
> **Believe a woman or an epitaph,**
> **Or any other thing that's false, before**
> **You trust in critics.**

Archbishop C. Garbett:

> **Any fool can criticise, and many of them do.**

M. J. C. Hodgart:

> **A critic is a haunter of unquiet graves. He tries to evoke the presence of a living art, but usually succeeds only in disturbing the peace of the dead.**

Dr. Johnson:

> **Criticism is a study by which men grow important and formidable at very small expense.**

Critics have also always been accused of living a parasitical existence, battening on the hard work of artists. Sir Henry Wootton:

> **Critics are like the brushers of noblemen's clothes.**

But no artist should take them too seriously. Robert Morley:

> **If the critics were always right we should be in deep trouble.**

But criticism does have a higher purpose than just depressing artists. Its moral function is to educate, by pointing up the deficiencies of the system, whether in politics or in art. Many critics take this rôle seriously and sincerely hope that their words will assist in the creation of a better system.

But the trouble is that a critic is in a position of power and will sometimes use that power to put across his own views at the expense of others. This can lead to repression. A critic of strong views who hates a certain book may put off people who would enjoy it. Perhaps there should be some other system for recommendations. A report from the *Edinburgh Evening News:*

> **Mrs. M. Steven suggests that the BBC mark items polluted by swearing, in the published programmes, by an asterisk, or, better still, a swastika, and so save people switching their sets on and off.**

"Put your shoulders back, you horrible little man—Get your hair cut—Pull yourself together, you pansy!"

That sort of idea, which sounds as if it's just offering free choice, is potentially dangerous, because it makes a moral judgment. It raises the whole issue of censorship. Some critics feel censorship to be part of their rôle, though usually censors come from other walks of life. News from the *Sunday Mirror:*

> **The censors appear to have little specialist knowledge of the theatre. Playwright Terence Feely tells me that he asked one of these gentlemen what he did before becoming a censor. He replied: 'They were very pleased with the way I handled the Trooping of the Colour arrangements, so they gave me this job.'**

There is always the danger that criticism may lead to intolerance. An opinion published in the old *News Chronicle:*

> **Yesterday somebody who should know about it told me the ancient Greeks were homosexuals. If so, they were a thoroughly bad lot. It's high time we banned Greek from our schools and universities.**

For every critic there's a danger of criticism giving way to prejudice. Another constant worry is that the critic is going to lose touch with his audience, in other words that he's going to talk over the heads of the very people he's trying to interest. Critics always seem a bit superior, but they can at times get hopelessly remote. Stephen Potter:

> **The critic must always be on top of, or better than, the person criticised.**

This danger of remoteness is even greater in academic circles, amongst university dons and lecturers. More from Stephen Potter:

> **Donmanship he defines as 'the art of criticising without actually listening'.**

Critics can get so involved in their rôle that they can't see the wood for the trees. A little verse by E. B. White:

> **The critic leaves at curtain fall**
> **To find, in starting to review it,**
> **He scarcely saw the play at all**
> **For watching his reaction to it.**

*"And now Mother's very cross indeed
with you!"*

Any sort of criticism depends on the ideas and preconceptions of the critic, but he must make some attempt to bridge the gap between his ideals and what the artist presents to him. G. K. Chesterton:

A great deal of contemporary criticism reads to me like a man saying: 'Of course I do not like green cheese; I am very fond of brown sherry.'

But few critics would phrase their views so simply. Many of them are guilty of gross over-writing, what Christopher Fry once referred to as:

The patter of tiny criticism.

Here's Laurence Sterne's view:

Of all the cants which are canted in this canting world – though the cant of hypocrites may be the worst – the cant of criticism is the most tormenting.

And an epigram by Samuel Butler – 'On Modern Critics':

**For daring nonsense seldom fails to hit,
Like scattered shot, and pass with some for wit.**

One of the perennial charges levelled at critics by artists is that they don't know anything about the subjects they discuss. Lord Byron again:

> A man must serve his time to every trade
> Save censure – critics all are ready made.
> Take hackneyed jokes from Miller, got by rote,
> With just enough of learning to misquote.

Here's Sir Herbert Beerbohm Tree's description of the critic, A. B. Walkely:

> **A whipper-snapper of criticism who quoted dead languages to hide his ignorance of life.**

It's not only in the world of art that such charges are made. Harold Macmillan:

> **I have never found in a long experience of politics, that criticism is ever inhibited by ignorance.**

And here's a remark by George Moore:

> **The lot of critics is to be remembered by what they failed to understand.**

As I suggested earlier, the reason for all this rudeness about critics is that most quotable writers have suffered at their hands and that, basically, no one likes being criticised. Somerset Maugham:

> **People ask you for criticism, but they only want praise.**

Mark Twain:

> **I like criticism, but it must be my way.**

There's a feeling among artists that critics are very good at disliking and not so good at praising their works. An anonymous rhyme:

> **When I did well, I heard it never;**
> **When I did ill, I heard it ever.**

The theatre is a world of spiky emotions and theatrical criticism often reflects this. It can get very bitchy. George Bernard Shaw:

> **A drama critic is a man who leaves no turn unstoned.**

Because of the transience of the medium, the business of a theatre critic is particularly difficult. John Mason Brown:

To many people dramatic criticism must seem like an attempt to tattoo soap bubbles.

To playwrights the presence of a critic presents another problem. Somerset Maugham:

How can you write a play of which the ideas are so significant that they will make the critic of *The Times* sit up in his stall and at the same time induce the shop-girl in the gallery to forget the young man who is holding her hand?

The reactions of the public should come first, but those reactions are often influenced by the opinions of critics. Adverse notices can kill a show stone-dead. Every theatrical production thrives on good reviews – like this one from the *Wimbledon Borough News:*

The whole cast can be congratulated on making a Shakespeare comedy really amusing.

A FIRST NIGHT.—*Indignant Playwright (to leading actor, behind the scenes).* " Confound it, man, you've absolutely murdered the piece!" *Leading Actor.* " Pardon me, but I think the foul play is yours!"

AT THE PREMIÈRE

Lady in Front Row (to her neighbour, towards the end of the second act). " Who is this man next me, who's just come in,—do you know ? He doesn't seem to be paying the smallest attention to the play ! "

Her Neighbour. " Oh, I expect he's a critic. He's probably made up his mind long ago what he's going to say of the piece; but he's just dropped in to *confirm his suspicions.*"

Here's another from the *Sale and Stretford Guardian:*

> **This week Altrincham Garrick present Chekhov's *The Seagull*, a play which does not do justice to a strong cast.**

Those are reasonably good notices; it's the other sort playwrights and actors fear and which give them such profound distrust of critics. P. G. Wodehouse:

> **Has anybody ever seen a drama critic in the daytime? Of course not. They come out after dark, up to no good.**

Literature is another area where critics wield a lot of power and can make or break a writer. A little verse by Thomas Hood:

What is the modern Poet's fate?
To write his thought upon a slate.
The Critic spits on what is done,
Gives it a wipe – and all is gone.

The writer rarely knows who will review his work and what that reviewer's preconceptions will be. It can be rather worrying. A review from the *Spectator:*

A reviewer must be honest. The present reviewer is
bound to confess that Miss ——'s book offends against
such taste as he has and such feelings as live in his mind
about the mystery of things. Why should Miss —— write
about ladies 'picking up their skirts and showing their
lovely legs to the men'?

At least Miss —— got her book read. It doesn't always happen. The Rev. Sydney Smith:

I never read a book before reviewing it; it prejudices one
so.

If you're looking for concise condemnation of a book by a critic, it's hard to better Dorothy Parker's famous comment on A. A. Milne's *The House at Pooh Corner* (she reviewed under the name 'Constant Reader'):

Tonstant Weader fwowed up.

This chapter has contained a lot of criticisms of critics, but not so far the one that is most commonly made by aggrieved artists. Here it is, succinctly expressed by Benjamin Disraeli:

You know what critics are? – the men who have failed in
literature and art.

Samuel Taylor Coleridge:

Reviewers are usually people who would have been
poets, historians, biographers, etc., if they could; they
have tried their talents at one or the other, and have
failed; therefore they turn critic.

Oliver Wendell Holmes:

> **Nature, when she invented, manufactured, and patented her authors, contrived to make critics out of the chips that were left.**

Much of this dislike is just the defence-mechanism of bruised egoes, but most artists do resent having their work criticised by someone who is less good at it than they themselves. This is not wholly fair on critics. Clayton Rawson:

> **Can't a critic give his opinion of an omelette without being asked to lay an egg?**

But artists suffer from just the same self-absorption as critics and get paranoid about criticism from a non-expert. In the words of Channing Pollock:

> **A critic is a legless man who teaches running.**

Or of Brendan Behan:

> **Critics are like eunuchs in a harem: they know how it's done, they've seen it done every day, but they're unable to do it themselves.**

I'll close the chapter – and indeed the book – with two further thoughts on criticism. First, an encouraging one from the composer, Sibelius:

> **Pay no attention to what the critics say; no statue has ever been put up to a critic.**

And, finally, a word of advice from Elbert Hubbard:

> **To avoid criticism, do nothing, say nothing, be nothing.**